I0415981

INCITE
Planetary Revolution

THE COLOR OF GOD
AND THE SUBSTANCE THEREOF

the rant of
syndax vuzz

This book is a work of fiction. Places, events, and situations in this story are purely fictional. Any resemblance to actual persons, living or dead, is coincidental.

ISBN: 1-4107-4354-3 (e-book)
ISBN: 1-4107-4355-1 (Paperback)

This book is printed on acid free paper.

1stBooks - rev. 08/21/03

Table of Contents

11/92

"WARNING TO HUMANITY"

"THE GREATEST PERIL IS TO BECOME TRAPPED IN SPIRALS OF ENVIRONMENTAL DECLINE, POVERTY AND UNREST LEADING TO SOCIAL, ECONOMIC AND ENVIRONMENTAL COLLAPSE. NO MORE THAN ONE OR A FEW DECADES REMAIN BEFORE THE CHANCE TO AVERT THE THREATS WE NOW CONFRONT WILL BE LOST AND THE PROSPECTS FOR HUMANITY IMMEASURABLY DIMINISHED."

from an appeal signed by more than
1500 distinguished scientists
from around the world
including
101 Nobel Prize winners

-The Union of Concerned Scientists-

word definitions are taken from
Webster's Ninth New Collegiate Dictionary

THIS IS FOR THE CHILDREN
FOR WHOSE ABDUCTION
FROM PARADISE
WE ARE ALL RESPONSIBLE

A MESSAGE IN A BOTTLE
ISSUED FORTH
FROM THE BOWELS OF SOCIETY

FOR THE COMMON MAN
WITH WHOM WE SHARE
A COMMON MIND

FOR THE WHOLE EARTH
WHICH IS SCREAMING OUT
THE PAIN OF MAN'S IGNORANCE

An apology

If my presentation appears crude, it is because I am only a common laborer unskilled in the art of communication. I hope that my passion for truth out weighs my unrefined quality of writing. Because I want my children to read this as soon as possible, it will be simple in essence, as easy to understand as I can make it, though I touch on topics uncommon, sometimes difficult to convey. I will be general rather than specific. I beg the indulgence of whatever "experts" or otherwise scholarly persons whom chance may cause to read.

THIS IS

PART OBSERVATION
PART WARNING
PART CHALLENGE
TO VERIFY OR DENY

BUT FOR THE MOST PART
IT IS A QUESTION UNANSWERED

AND AN INVITATION
TO EXPLORE FOR ONESELF
THE FACTS OF LIFE
AND THEIR SIGNIFICANCE

THE FOUNDATION

FOR PLANETARY REVOLUTION

IS LAID

WITHIN OUR COMMON MIND

Its a subject we rarely mention, if ever, the condition of the world and our relationship to it. Yet it is the single most important topic there is, personal problems not withstanding, because it is out of these conditions and relationships that our personal problems grow. Perhaps on occasion, various aspects of what is happening may arise in conversation- the wars, the threats of war, the preparation for war, the destruction and poisoning of the land, water and air, the economic and social injustice resulting in poverty, starvation, disease, violence and death. Yes, sometimes we may broach a topic or two, and when we do, we have various opinions, invariably conflicting to one degree or another. One will quote the latest theory in vogue in the media or among intellectuals or in one's own particular social group. Or one will repeat a cliche voiced by the parental figures of one's childhood frequently repeated- "If its not one thing its another, that's just the way it is, human nature, it will never change." Or another may venture a simple observation of fact.

Yet, in our discussions, however deep or shallow they may be, there is no passion to go to the end, to discover the truth. We are confused human beings, living in fear, each pursuing his own narrow desire with a brain which has been conditioned through hundreds of thousands of years to survive by violence and competition, and molded through a lifetime of the past ignorance being pounded in each day from every direction by various "authorities" - parental, educational, religious, social and legal.

THE CAUSE OF TRUTH AND JUSTICE

The intention of this work is
To do that which is good,
in the sense of
fertile, bountiful, suitable, attractive,
free from disease,
wholesome and true.

The intention of this work is
To do that which is right,
in the sense of
straight, direct, and real.

It is our right
-in the sense of-
something to which one has a just claim,
something that one may properly claim as due.

To right
-to adjust to the proper condition-

This message is addressed to the common woman and man.

Common in the sense of
relating to the whole community,
characterized by a lack of privilege,
shared by all.

This message is for those who labor.

labor in the sense of
spending one's life energy,
physically and mentally,
in difficult, compulsory, strenuous, and painful work
to provide the goods and services
required by society.

This is for the most common people of the Earth, whose labor is exploited for profit by the least common people who hold the power, position, and privilege of managing the world's material abundance.

The warrior, too, here is addressed.

Warrior in the sense of
a person engaged in some struggle or conflict.

This work is to suggest there is something wrong,
fundamentally wrong,
with the whole of human activity of the earth today.

Wrong in the sense of
not right or proper, not according to truth or facts, not satisfactory, not in accordance with one's needs, without regard for what is proper or just.

Wrong in the sense of
unjust and outrageous injury, inhumane imposing of burdens one cannot endure, exacting more than one can perform, a relentless and unremitting subjection to annoyance and suffering, suffering caused by an infringement of rights.

This work is to suggest that the most significant step
in the evolution of man is occurring now

-evolution being a process in which the whole universe is a
progression of interrelated phenomena, a process of
continuous change from a lower, simpler, or worse to a
higher, more complex, or better state.-

mankind's role in this process
-now-
is to bring about immediately
an immense, global, sudden,
radical, complete change.

planetary revolution

We have arrived at the turning point. This is it, here and now. A sudden, immense, immediate, complete, radical, global change. No wealth, power, position or privilege, nor any particular or special physical or intellectual capacity will allow an escape from this planetary revolution. Every aware human being sees that the world is in an unprecedented, rapidly expanding state of deterioration. This is a fact. The human being is at the center and is the driving force of this crisis.

The population explosion plus the explosion of technology have created problems that seem to be beyond the scope of man's ability to solve, problems that threaten to turn the planet into a ball of flame, either through the use of nuclear weapons or the greenhouse effect, if we do not first foul, waste, or otherwise destroy the planetary life support system of land, water, and air.

Equally significant, if not more so, is the ancient evil of man's inhumane treatment of his fellow man, which is the dominant thread of our worldwide social fabric. Every form of violence, whether it is subtle- such as competition, greed, envy, apathy, prejudice, rumor, etcetera, - or gross- such as rips and burns flesh, breaks and crushes bone, and ruptures internal organs, - or utterly evil- such as slavery, every form of violence is the norm, a way of life, accepted by all, but a very few.

At the present rate of progress, less than 20 years will have brought us to the end of civilization as we now know it. Awareness of this fact must penetrate the consciousness of mankind in order for the population of the Earth to act as one, all one, for we alone are responsible. There is no other to save us.

There is no authority that will solve all our problems- not from the political, religious, or scientific arenas, nor from outer space, nor from the past or future, nor from heaven or hell. There is no conspiracy of do-gooders to change things from behind the scenes. No unknown mystic poet saint will rise from the masses to save the world. Nor is there an inner authority hidden within our brain, waiting to be let out and take charge. We have created this society which is destroying itself and fouling the environment. We create it, all of us together, each moment, with our thought, which determines our behavior- minute by minute, hour upon hour, day after day, year in and year out.

The manner in which the human brain now functions is the wellspring of man's sorrow. It produces our personal problems and collectively we have produced the present state of the planet. (Yes, the human brain has created many good and wonderful things. But it is not the good that now dominates the world.)

The initiator of human behavior is a genetic survival mechanism of the human brain, passed down to us by our ancient ape-like ancestors. This mechanism, which came into being to ensure the survival of the individual, now controls the whole of human life.

As a guarantor of personal survival there is no equal. Human beings have increased their number in the last one hundred years from one and a half billion to five billion. Man has become the overwhelmingly dominant species on the planet. We have not only explored and mapped the whole planet, we have visited the moon several times. Our influence has altered every aspect of life on Earth. Animals, plants, and microbes are being domesticated, produced, reproduced, and genetically altered or manipulated. We have increased and accelerated the extinction of species alarmingly. (Do we consider homo sapiens invulnerable?)

Our Knowledge and our tools, which originated as vague memories combined with sticks and stones, have developed to a degree limited only by our imagination. We have increased our speed of travel one thousand times in the last one hundred years. We have increased our speed and distance of communication ten million times. Technological miracles in science, medicine, industry, agriculture, computation, recreation, personal convenience, and entertainment are now commonplace, every day occurrences, taken for granted and often abused by those few who may be privileged enough to partake of them.

Meanwhile, the vast majority of us lack a meaningful education, relevant to the actual, sorrowful experience of the whole of human life, or even adequate food, clothing, and shelter, much less an opportunity to appreciate the significance of life.

All too often, for far too many of us, our daily life appears to be an unending series of problems. Our ability to maintain our health and our sanity is taxed to the limit and beyond. Life seems to be a struggle of sorrow ending in death. Our love and our joy is fleeting, hollow, tainted. This aspect of life is part of the basic structure of the human brain. It is so because of the natural evolution of life.

Suffering is not only an attitude or point of view or a particular set of circumstances, but a natural consequence of the over development of that part of the brain that demands we survive.

This brain structure naturally channels our life's energy into a particular direction which is, ultimately and absolutely, a dead end.

This is so simply because there is only so much one can do to avoid death.

Let's begin again.

The whole of life on planet Earth calls forth a symbol from the human brain.

If you do not allow your automatic defense mechanisms to reject it out of hand as too broad or general or naively mystic, visionary, new age, etc., or too intrusive on your private fantasies or fears- you will find there is an immediate, intense energy, an utter urgency that exists within the phrase 'planetary revolution'.

It may be the most significant symbol created by man because it symbolizes the most significant event of this phase of evolution.

Even the least aware among us senses on a primal level an atmosphere of impending doom. This is an observation born of an intimate contact with an unprecedented magnitude of human sorrow and it's manifestations which are exploding the world over.

The global society
in which we find ourselves
is in constant conflict
between divisions of people.

While we attempt to ignore the facts, they are relentlessly intruding upon our consciousness through the mass media and in our families, neighborhoods, nations, and every level of community. This is necessary to the process of human evolution regardless of how painful it becomes. The necessity lies not in the degree of suffering that we experience, rather, it is necessary that the old forms and patterns of human relationship end. It is not necessary to feel pain in bringing about the transformation of the world- unfortunately it is often only extreme pain and fear that calls our attention to crisis.

Then, too, there are those, so stultified by luxury, so insulated from the vagaries of living, that extreme pain constitutes not being able to take that European vacation or not being able to buy a new car every year or keep every hair in place or make it to the country club on time.

The structure of our banally evil society is collapsing of it's own weight and no one can/will/should stop it. What emerges from the soil of ruin is what we are preparing the way for now. What we may do is rise up, deconstruct the old world and create a new one, using what is good and discarding what is not.

The change is coming, the question is - will we be crushed or will we become wholly conscious of what is happening and what we need to create?

BOOK ONE

PRELUDE

SCIENCE AND TECHNOLOGY
THE NEW MYTHOLOGY

Of presupposition
paradigms, programs, and prejudice

our attitude
what it is
where it comes from

Its as necessary to understand the fundamental implications of evolution as it was once necessary to understand the implications of the Earth being round.

EVOLUTION I

out of darkness
universal creation
born in blinding light

primordial atom
divides into elements
creating space and time

matter in motion
a progression of interrelated phenomena
a process of continuous change
from a lower, simpler, or worse
to a higher, more complex, or better state

over eons
stars, planets, solar systems, and galaxies
form, revolve around each other
dissolve and reform

and immense chunk of rock
revolving and orbiting a star
comes into being
from an infinite number of influences
which span the universe
from the first moment of creation

a fire ignites within the rock
cracking it open like an egg
releasing gases and molten rock
creating atmosphere, ocean, and island

electrical storms bond atoms in the atmosphere
into the molecules of amino acids and nucleotides
-the building blocks of living matter-

these biological molecules
fall into the primordial stew
which is the surface of the Earth

over the span of a billion years
a strange molecule forms
-the replicator-

a molecule that creates copies of itself
a primitive ancestor of the control center of every living cell of every
living thing on the planet
the DNA molecule
the essential mechanism of life

Simply because these facts are so basic to the world we live in and because they so intimately and powerfully determine our existence- what we are suggesting is the essence of the scientific view in broad and general terms. Of course, scientific knowledge only goes so far- it can't explain what "caused" the big bang and it can't prove what "caused" replication. It can only symbolize, measure, and compare aspects of observable phenomena.

-a note on natural selection-

-The natural process that results in the survival of individuals or groups best adjusted to the conditions under which they live and that is equally important for the perpetuation of desirable genetic qualities and for the elimination of undesirable ones as they are produced by genetic recombination or mutation.-

Natural selection is just another term for the physical laws of matter and energy. Its like the rules established in the first moment of time brought forth stars, galaxies, and planets- raw, pure, and awesomely powerful nature decrees the form life takes just as much as our DNA does. Life arose out of the continual flowing movement of stimulus and response between matter and energy in space over time and out of the continual flowing movement of information between probing replicators and the environment they found themselves in. All forms of life fit their environment like a key fits a lock.

REPLICATION

The original matter of life and death.

a molecule that reproduces itself
sometimes makes mistakes
creating not itself
but a variation

over the course of a billion years
-essentially an eternity in human terms-
the number of replicators
and variations thereof
exploded exponentially
and hyperdimensionally
within the confines of competition

3

Among a countless number of a variety of replicators, the molecular building blocks in the ancient oceans became increasingly scarce and more valuable. Certain types of replicators survived and became more numerous while others became less numerous or extinct. Replicators that could break up other replicators and use the freed building blocks for themselves set the standard of ruthless selfishness for the process of natural selection that brought forth the human being.

Here emerges the first prejudice-
the human perspective.

competition- active demand by two or more organisms or kinds of organisms for some environmental resources in short supply.

to compete- to strive consciously or unconsciously for an objective

Remember- until human beings came along there was no such happenings as "demands", "strivings", or "desires"- there was no meaning or purpose. The universe- space and time- matter in motion- just existed according to its own innate properties and laws. The universe and life unfolded as one infinitely long, extraordinarily complex physical, chemical, and biological reaction. Life was unconscious. It did not "want" to evolve. It did not "seek" more abundant life or "chase" objectives of higher value like greater mobility or more flexible adaptations or keener sense.

Bearing that in mind, we may proceed with the terminology that best describes the appearance of events- as if the universe were acting with a will that passionately desired the evolution of life.

Replicators acquired walls within which they gathered materials for their reproduction and were protected from the environment. These cells were so successful, replicators without walls became extinct.

With the ability to store, process, and consume food within the cell membrane, the replicators grew larger and more powerful, becoming the architect and engineer for every living form we see- deoxyribonucleic acid- DNA.

Plant cells appeared first, living off sunshine and ocean by way of green chlorophyll, producing oxygen as a waste product. Animal cells came along consuming the oxygen which provided a greater concentration of energy, allowing the animal to seek its food more aggressively and outrun its enemies more quickly.

Cells learned to adhere, one to another, for the enhanced survival aspects- a member of a group might die but the organism as a whole lived. Organizations of cohesive cells flourished, opening the door to the next step of evolution- specialization through the division of labor. The division of labor allowed for a more complex organism. Some cells would form a protective covering, the forerunner of skin, some would process food and oxygen, which became guts and lungs, other cells would become sensitive to light, vibrations, or chemicals which developed into our senses of touch, sight, hearing, smell, and taste.

Thus these multi-celled creatures became the next dominant form of life, with their increasing ability to hunt food, avoid danger, grow and reproduce. Over the span of a billion years the multi-celled life formed a primitive worm up to two feet long- another billion years and man will arrive. The pace of evolution is constant acceleration.

The worm evolves into fish. Shrinking oceans and expanding land evolved fish into amphibian into reptile. For a time dinosaurs ruled the Earth but their small brains and cold-bloodedness didn't allow them to adapt to dramatic climatic changes. They became extinct and mammals inherited the Earth.

In order to make up for their lack of size and strength in a world dominated by dinosaurs, mammals had developed proportionately larger brains.

Of the mammals that inherited the Earth, the ones that lived in trees advanced evolution- from squirrels to monkeys to apes. They had to develop hands to grip tree branches and binocular vision to jump from branch to branch. Most of all these tree dwellers had to develop their brains. Split second mental computations had to come into play in order to calculate distances, wind speeds, branch movements, and body balance along with a keen memory of past experiences with acrobatic stunts.

Again nature forces the hand of evolution through drier weather which formed expanded clearings in the forest. The apes came out of the trees and stood up to look across the savannas of tall grass. Picking up rocks and sticks to hunt food and kill his enemies the first hominid creates tools and begins his domination of the planet.

Over vast amounts of time, billions of years and thousands upon thousands of generations of DNA molecules, with only two overriding concerns- survival and reproduction- evolve through environmental pressures from one-celled life into a human being.

While the DNA molecule evolved from the stellar dust of the big bang.

EVOLUTION II

Our Deepest Nature

To Live

to pursue pleasure and avoid pain
to grow, expand, and reproduce
to seek more abundant life

and to cheat death
the highest glory

Is Built Into Our Muscle, Blood, and Bone

not only on the molecular and cellular levels
but by implication, inference, and insight
on the sub-atomic and astrophysical levels as well

Five million years ago post-ape pre-man comes out of the forest and begins to stand erect so that he may watch for danger, in the process he frees his hands from walking to carry food, use tools, and communicate. He gathers food from the ground, hunts insects and small game, and scavenges. He learns to fashion higher quality tools from appropriate rock for which he searches miles, takes home and crafts and uses repeatedly over time. At four foot tall and seventy pounds, with a fist sized brain, he had no great size or strength, no horns, claws, or fangs- yet he was able to compete favorably with the big cats, the dominant predators.

After about three million years man evolves a bigger brain and body- though physically he is about as big as us- his brain is only about half the size of ours. He begins to experiment with speech, culture, and social organization. The growth of man's brain accelerates, his language becomes more articulate, he controls fire and cooks food and his stone tools and weapons are of ever higher quality. He strives to understand and explain life and explore his world.

About a million years ago the growth rate of the human brain exploded until it reached its present size a hundred thousand years ago. Human behavior became less instinctive and more adaptable to changing conditions and more adept at exploiting resources- undoubtedly due to the greater number of brain cells.

More brain cells allows better memory capacity and more complex mental circuits necessary for learning, storing, and communicating knowledge. The individual who demonstrated better ingenuity,

6

improvisation, imagination, and invention- the individual who could best think- was selected by nature to live longer and reproduce more.

With environmental pressures and increasing brain size, mental activity exploded, becoming more powerful and influential in the world and at the same time more subtle and refined in it's machinations. Through thought- the storing of ever greater numbers of images, for greater lengths of time and recalling the images with greater speed, accuracy, and relevance, and the establishment of corresponding sounds-language- symbols not only for people, things, and events but also for desires, emotions, measurements, predictions, and plans concerning the future, detections of pattern and comparisons of quality and all manner of ideas- the mind of man begins to replace DNA as the determinate of human evolution.

Knowledge became the primary premium resource available to humans. Culture took over evolution from nature. We began to evolve, at an explosive pace, better and better survival skills from learning and sharing knowledge within the family and tribe from generation to generation rather than through reproductive variations or genetic recombinations or mutations that take at least hundreds of thousands of years. Cultural selection is what is at work in the world now. The mechanics and techniques of cultural selection (which are basically the same as natural selection only faster and more powerful) maybe nearing the end of their contribution to the progression of evolution. Pure perception may cut to the core of what makes for the best in life rather than the trial and error process of thought.

culture is information
-social and technological-
shared and used

information is a mental process
-memory-
an electrochemical process of brain cells
a memory is a specific neural firing pattern

the whole of thought is memory
and variations thereof

In it's primal essence thought is memory, an electrochemical process of brain cells, images and ideas stored in the brain, neural firing patterns. Memory can be attributed to matter and energy following the laws of physics and the memory stored in a strand of DNA is cosmic in proportion. Memory is the primal tool of replication. The DNA remembers itself and how it came to be and that memory is the course it's life follows. In this sense DNA is simply a form of memory.

Nature selected first, memories that avoided death longer and that reproduced more often with greater accuracy. The competition became more stiff and survival machines were built by DNA. It is here, from the cellular level on up, that the avoidance of death becomes more dramatic. It has been observed in the simplest forms of life and becomes more blatantly obvious the more sophisticated the nervous system- "nature red in tooth and claw"- the primal memory for avoiding death, the animal instinct for survival translated as human emotion- FEAR.

This primeval fear is built into all life as a simple mechanism for sensing and responding to life threats. It is the "animal instinct" built into our brain. This is the hardware- and of course the software- knowledge, tradition, culture, belief- is designed to fit the hardware. The code that the brains programs are written in is language- gesture, sound, speech, syntax. Thinking and language evolved together. Language sharpened and clarified thought. The more precisely defined our description of the world, the greater the potential for our manipulation and exploitation of the environment. Our desires, instincts, and emotions remain essentially the same as our pre-civilized ancestors. What sets us apart is the product of thought.

the machine of perception
the biological computer
the human brain

Our senses are the means by which we interact with the world.
Without the input provided by our senses,
we have no basis for the response necessary to meet our needs.
The human brain uses stored sense perceptions
-memory-knowledge-culture-
as the fundamental response tool of survival.
Prior to an ability to order the thinking process
through specific symbols,
whether visual, auditory, mental, or otherwise-
an initial focal point for the bundle of sense perceptions,
both stored and immediate-
the basis on which to store and retrieve memory,
the pivot upon which to anchor belief,
the fulcrum upon which to weigh choice,
the foundation upon which to base distinctions-
coalesced into an intensely potent
sensory/emotion/thought
psychic, physical, social phenomena of the human brain-
the self
me, myself, and I

This "I" is the first discreet, concrete movement of thought- all thought is simply an extension of this initial movement.

The First Division

OK- Let's be clear what we're talkin' 'bout.

Its like pre-man was not quite conscious. His behavior was motivated entirely by glandular secretions and instinct. The increased number of brain cells in the seat of the senses- the mind of man- following it's biological imperative, began to reach out and pay an intense attention to the whole of life. The energy generated by the full blown human sensory apparatus- our entire nervous system-coalescing and concentrating in the brain cells, sends those neurons firing out of control, beyond their boundaries of basic survival patterns.

This is the birth of the sense of self and with the sense of self arose the world as an object of perception, manipulation, and organization. This is the birth of our human semi-consciousness.

in the beginning was the word
specifying and ordering thought
identifying and symbolizing
people, things, and events
by way of division

The translation of perception into symbol is division.
The initial division necessary
for any symbolic representation
of any aspect of the world
is between the self and the world.
Me, here and the world, there.
Its like "this" and like "that".

This is the structure and function of the machine of division.
-" | "-
dividing "me" from the environment
sets the stage
for the division of the world
allowing "me" to act in the world
from a dimension beyond
the glandular, instinctive animal reaction

the Human Brain and it's Thought Processes
Born of the Fear of Death

BOOK TWO
Evolution III

OUR COMMON MIND

The seeds of the human brain were scattered through the cosmos by the big bang and were planted in this solar system as the Earth. The human being grew out of the planet like a blade of grass through concrete, seeking the sunlight of a universal intelligence.

That intelligence which informed the energy that guided matter through space and time is the same intelligence that brings us forth.

The imperative of understanding human origins is the imperative of understanding ourselves in the world now. Not just your self or my self, but the self of our common mind, which now controls the world, and includes each personal self.

in that first moment of creation
aspects of mind arose
order, stability, pattern, symmetry
apparent purpose
sense
the mechanism of perception
as in action and reaction, stimulus and response
paradox, duality, polarity

Mind is the evolution of matter in the universe.

The Universal Mind formed matter into man.

A hundred thousand years ago the fully human being was created whole, brain and body. Over the course of seventy five thousand years mankind, in it's infancy, begins to divide it's perceptions into memories and names creation. About twenty five thousand years ago specialized knowledge and technique, art, and religion are being conceived and born. The emergence of the first civilizations began only five thousand years ago- as noted by advanced techniques in agriculture, engineering, architecture, metal, wood, and stone work, powerful governments, expanded populations, universal religions, written language, literature, music, dance, drama, painting, poetry, sculpture, law and war.

The human being came out of the animal just as surely as you came out of your mother's womb.

our brain and body
a vast conglomeration of accumulated memories
built up by natural selection
engineered by the DNA molecule
dating back to the beginning of time

The animal we came out of is completely determined by heredity and environment. It acts in only one way- with an automatic response according to its genetic programming. The human body- which includes the brain- is animal. Straight up, its OK. We couldn't have got here any other way. The fact is we are driven by genetic and biological programs so powerful- eating and reproducing and the world history they have created- that it is sometimes hard to see, other than our tools, just what it is that separates us from the animal.

but that's enough in itself
our tools, our knowledge, out technique
-culture-

though we are animal bone deep
we possess an innate ability
to transcend space and time
by virtue of our brain
through insight and technology

insight- the power or act of seeing into a situation : penetration
the act or result of apprehending the inner nature of things : discernment

insight is
the catalyst
of consciousness

an event
the significance of which is
comparable to the big bang and replication

At present we are only semi-conscious,
our life's energy being wasted
by the self
in the pursuit of an impossibility.

the seat of the senses
in the process of perception
contacts the world
with it's habitual neural firing patterns

the influx of extra energy
generated by an intense
unceasing observation
of the environment

sends those neurons firing
through the vast surplus
of newly acquired brain cells
outside the limits
of the genetic
and environmental
conditioning

producing the initial insights
in the mind of man

That's the birth of what makes us human.
Homo sapiens were born whole.
The earliest men were like infants,
innocent and unschooled,
fully human,
only less sophisticated than we.

The earliest insights of man were like magic-
a gift of the gods.

Their ideas and inventions,
of gods and demons,
and agriculture, metal, and math,
were far more momentous for mankind
than any of the theories and technologies
we come up with today.

We are at the tail end of an evolutionary phase they began.
They produced a world of which we are the product.

The primal, fundamental human insights
were not a product of man,
were not a product of the self.

They were a product of the universal mind-
a manifestation of the highest, most complex
interaction of matter and energy
apparent in the universe.

The seed of insight was sown in the first moment of time.
Matter formed into man
and looked at itself
and saw that it was good.

The primal, fundamental insights
became memory and formed the core paradigm of human thought.
-the self-

it is out of perception that insight is born

In the Garden of Eden, Eve Tempts and Adam Tastes.

In the first fully human perception was the key to the universe.
We could see the world and our self,
and we could see ourselves in the world,
and that ourselves in the world was one small part
of an awesome, immeasurable, living whole
that fit together, perfectly, like a special blessing.

The perception was perfection,
we knew life was an astonishing mystery
and that it was good absolutely.

Its like the ultimate pleasure
and as soon as the animal within us,
the flesh,
our brain centered nervous system,
experienced a sense of absolute goodness,
it feared the ending of that sense-
selfishly it didn't want to let go
and the experience was committed to memory,
an aspect of the self,
a part of the past.

Interlude I

POLARITY

a quality of the universe
woven into the fabric of physical law
that makes sense perception possible

In considering the evolution of life, a process of increasing order and complexity, we must recognize it's inseparable counterpart- de-evolution or decay. Its just like you can't die without living or live without dying. Its just like our whole mode of linear language/thought in which virtually any idea expressed implies or contains it's opposite. They appear mutually exclusive, but it is only in the imagination that positive can exist separately from negative. In actuality they define each other, simultaneously, different aspects of one whole.

The Polarity Paradox
Life and Death
Dividing the World
Good and Evil

Here we acknowledge that old devil- duality
mind and matter
Inherent in symbolizing sense perceptions
predator and prey
management and labor
master and slave
Though they appear in diametric opposition
pleasure and pain
They are aspects of one whole
male and female
One is not known without the other
future and past
Which implies syntax
subject and object
And drives our logic
cause and effect
And breeds technique
action and reaction
stimulus and response
perception-experience-thought
All occurs within a spectrum of polar awareness.

15

Adam Swallows and Digests the Forbidden Fruit.

Selfishness, violence, greed, fear, hatred,
the devil,
-whatever you want to call it-
was the polar extreme of the *memory* of the absolute goodness
born of a whole perception
giving birth to our basic insights.

Its because implicit in seeing ourselves and the world
and seeing ourselves as an inseparable facet of the world,
we knew death was at hand for all living beings-
and death is what we have spent the last four billion years avoiding
with every ounce of our energy (matter, space, and time).

Knowledge, produced by insight, captured by thought,
-memory-
-the self-
is an extension of the animal instinct for survival-
so extensive, in fact,
that absolute physical and material security is now technologically
available.

As the same extension emotionally and psychologically
man creates god
out of fear.

Just as the infant learns that sense objects have an existence
independent of her perception, early man came to believe the
unperceived cause and forces of the world had their own independent
existence, and that these forces could be manipulated for her own benefit
via magic, religion, and ritual.

Out of the observation of the world man created syntax- subject-verb-
object- born of the symbolization of the cause and effect appearance of
matter in motion.

This syntax is the code that orders our world. This is the foundation of
knowledge. It implies a vast past and an apparent future intimately bound
to the present moment.

This syntax implies god as beginning and end, cause and effect all
rolled into one whole.

Thought created the idea of god to answer the impossible question
and superseded direct perception of the fact.

what it is

replication
-echo-reverberation-copy-reproduction-
and/or
the action or process of reproducing

culture
-the integrated pattern of human knowledge, belief, and behavior
that depends on man's capacity for learning
and transmitting knowledge to succeeding generations-

ergo

it is the nature
of the human brain
to produce insight
and cultivate knowledge

knowledge produces
great physical and psychological gratification
with it's corresponding
deprivation, destruction, and decadence

insight reveals
one
whole
living
world
working in perfect harmony

it goes somethin' like this here:
thought works kinda like a machine
the hardware of the brain
forms the structure of thought
runnin' on automatic
senses contact particular facet of the world
-division of perception-
triggers memory
-knowledge, program, prejudice-
(culture)
equals reaction
-in favor of personal benefit-
(selfish)
with the occasional flash of insight
-brought about by sustained attention-
that reveals the true connection between different facets of the world
which becomes the new knowledge
and on and on
from stargazer to star flight

Basic human thought processes extend themselves through observation, introspection, and the sharing of knowledge based upon a mechanism of replication that takes place in human brains and produces our common mind.

Knowledge, ideas, belief, culture, presupposition, programs, and prejudice- the whole of thought- consumes our common consciousness (and look at our global human behavior).

Thought, as an electrochemical process of replication taking place as neural firing patterns of human brain cells, has had an evolution of it's own.

Thought symbolizes the world, memory retains the pattern in the brain, and there that image replicates and variegates and successful variations (ones that lead to more abundant life) dominate the environment of the human mind.

Insight propels knowledge forward from the individual to the collective. The evolution of thought has been one of constant acceleration by way of culture and culture is the manifestation of our common mind.

OUR COMMON MIND REVISITED

95% of human history
occurred without benefit
of universal laws
or the one all commanding god

Human beings lived tribal magic
in a world of mysterious forces
and invisible beings
and everything in the world
was inhabited by spirits
with whom we might communicate.

The universe, having essentially perfected the animal in the form of homo sapiens, set the stage for the next phase of evolution-consciousness.

The semi-consciousness that has emerged on the planet is as yet dominated by the animal aspect of ourselves- fear- the primal memory to avoid death- at it's evolutionary peak- thought-culture-technique-the self-me, myself, and I.

in the beginning was the word
but what the word came out of
and what the word appears in
is our common consciousness
-it requires more than one brain-

Each brain functions fundamentally the same way
-thought seeking security-
regardless of any particular culture or conditioning.

But no brain has functioned,
no brain can function,
in isolation.
-No individual is *completely* alienated from the whole-
Every person who has survived childhood
has been thoroughly programmed
through social and environmental interaction.

Communication is the thread that binds human organization and social structure.

For a hundred thousand years prehistoric man lived in tribes of fifty to a hundred and fifty people consisting of generations of families and their dependents- evidence of our predisposition for cooperation. Their existence was a life and death struggle in which each day of survival, of testing the limits of their physical and mental capacities, of hunting and killing game, cooked over an open fire, eaten at home where resided your mate and offspring among other closely related families provided an almost ultimate and absolute satisfaction, each day full and sufficient unto itself.

This tribal existence allowed human beings to best meet their needs through living a communal lifestyle, all resources being shared equally.

This structure allowed for a natural justice. The tribe's people, in order for their small society to function efficiently, adhered to the highest ethical and moral standards of behavior. This was not a result of laws, police, judges, jails, politicians, preachers or priests who controlled behavior by physical or psychological force. It came about through the direct life experience of people living together with a simple, common goal- to be fed and sheltered and to procreate.

It did not occur to the tribe's people to keep track of who shared what with whom, where, when, and how much as we do today, down to the exact dollar, hour, weight, size, shape and quality of whatever goods and services we exchange. In the tribe it paid better to give and be generous with whatever you did and had, whether hunting, fishing, gathering, fashioning clothes, building shelters, or making tools and weapons, so that whatever you might need would come back around your way.

In these social structures there were no masters and slaves, beggars and thieves, police and criminals, judges and juries. Each person knew that the well-being of the whole tribe was the whole focus of life, creating the maximum amount of actual security possible, for both the individual and the group equally, simultaneously. The tribe's people knew not private property. The land, water, plants, and animals were for all. In cases of need personal possessions were freely exchanged. In cases of aberrant social behavior a natural justice would ostracize perpetrators- whether voluntarily or violently, temporarily or permanently- destructive personalities could not be long tolerated.

Without laws, police, judges, or jails to enforce commands there was no single, all powerful leader. Leaders grew into their roles naturally according to skills possessed. You would follow the lead of the best hunter when pursuing game. You would follow the lead of the best craftsmen when building shelter, making clothes, tools, or weapons. No one person's opinions would necessarily carry more weight than the rest of the tribe in common matters. Although there is an innate "pecking order" discernible in social encounters, it is genetic and biological, generally uncontested, except for ritualized combat/play among males vying for females, while cultural selection creates it's own order. Tribal life was a strictly cooperative venture.

The leadership aspects which arose came from those who worked hardest and longest and were the most generous with the fruit of their labor and intellect. Those who possessed these qualities would naturally capture and maintain the attention of the whole tribe in general on a daily basis.

The significance of this fact can hardly be overestimated as it would feed a deep seated human need- perhaps the most powerful need after food and sex that humans experience.

Human beings require love.

If there was any status associated with a particular occupation in the tribe, it was afforded the hunters and the healers. Of all foods man naturally craves meat most- try going seven days without any meat. The production of meat held a particular private pleasure and a public glory, both biologically as a concentration of vital nutrients and psychologically as image inflation from attention and appreciation. Among the hunters themselves, the ability to organize the hunt and the display of ruthless efficiency in killing- a matter of life and death- would command a peculiar power- violence and fear.

And the medicine woman, the tribe's connection to the spirit world, associated with the major human events- birth, illness, rites of passage, death, ostracizing of aberrant social behavior, and supplicant of the gods- credited with whatever benefits might accrue- health, abundant food, luck in battle, and the cooperation of nature.

if there was any status
associated with a particular gender
than it was afforded that half of humanity
which touches upon the divine

-the female-

after all
what is it
that is universally worshipped
by all men
regardless of
tribal, religious, or national affiliation?

the original deity
-the goddess-

it does not require
any cultural sophistication
to know
that the whole of life
comes into the world
through the body of a woman

***

and the exploiters of our aesthetic sense
the artists and the craftsmen
held the real magic
initiating the next dimension of evolution
by observing, thinking, creating
they cultivated awareness and technique
and transmitted them through the tribe
over generations
actions no longer determined strictly by
physical, chemical, and biological reactions

aesthetic perceptions and material skills
became psychological programs
and innumerable variations thereof
culture and technology

THE MIND OF THE CHILD

The human organism/infant associates goodness/love with the meeting of her needs- which later evolves into the satisfaction of her psychological desire. Our sense of goodness grew out of the dependency of the parent-offspring relationship- family. Relationships and conditions that fulfill our fundamental needs are good, ones that deprive us our well-being or our sense of security are not. As the organism develops, it seeks the same sense from the community- communication and cooperation or alienation and violence- according to it's own particular conditioning.

With the awareness of what is good and what is not arose a sense of *quality*, an appreciation of goodness and beauty in form and function- our aesthetic sense- seeking to make life better, more secure, more pleasurable. It is this emerging consciousness of a spectrum of quality that focuses our attention intensely upon our mental processes, images and ideas, in order to measure and compare any or all aspects of the world- past, present, and future- within the mind, seeking ever the highest quality.

This is the new dimension of complexity in the interaction of matter/energy in space/time- whole worlds may be contained, dissected, and recreated within the human brain. It is no longer necessary for evolution to spend lifetimes experimenting for the perfect way of life. Now life can cut to the chase. What once took generations to establish-better survival skill, ability, and the potential thereof- now may take place in hours or days with our high technology.

The sacred seed has split. The growth within pulsates and hesitates, sensing the world- if one thing or idea or action is better than another-what is the best?

this is the end
of Eden and innocence
and the beginning of
responsibility
public and private
local and global

Simple survival is no longer sufficiently satisfactory. For man, the whole process of life is far more vast than the indulgence of his appetite.

OUR COMMON MIND III

Sex, Hunger, and War
Environmental Resources
and the Basic Unit of Society
-the Family-

The whole focus of human life is to meet our interconnected biological and psychological needs. The more we are able to meet our biological needs, the greater the role our psychological need plays in life. Of course our psychological need is rooted in and is an extension of our biological need for food and sex. The programs we follow to fulfill our needs are culture and all it's variations.

Culture is transmitted first through our mother's breast.

It is evident in the simplest forms of life and becomes more apparent the more sophisticated the nervous system- as part of a process of replication, the parent-offspring relationship, our genetic predisposition for human contact, cooperation and communication or more precisely-love.

The skeleton of every human persona is created whole at a very early age and every person spends the rest of her life fleshing it out.

Parents create copies of themselves- automatically- there is no other way- we are genetic physically and its a genetic apparatus that generates, transmits, and receives culture- the human brain- our common mind.

Talk about the mirror of human relationship! When you look at your children and their behavior, you are looking deep into your own soul.

That's the way it is. The only way it could have turned out like this is for the universe to have evolved just so. Starting with nothing, then, wonder of wonders, self-replicating entities out of the big bang and out of replicators, consciousness, the miracle of astonishment.

The universe, life and death, evolution- its a never ending movement. What came before changes into what we are now and now we are creating what will be. Whether we know it or not, whether we like it or not, we are responsible for the world.

rather than die
a cell divides

during the process of division
two specific life forms
depend utterly on each other

-the genetic foundation
for the biological fact
of our social relationship-

24

cells that divide and are separate organisms
yet remain attached after division is complete
form multicellular organisms

the well being of the whole organism
becomes the function of each individual cell

the organization of cells
evolves an ever increasing ability
to cooperate and survive

the nature of life
to cooperate and depend
is as real and as significant
as the very tissue that forms the physical body

The tendency towards cooperation is the polar extreme of the tendency towards ruthless selfishness and is the more powerful, otherwise life would not have evolved. The driving force of survival- the fear of death- ruthless selfishness- by itself, is ultimately a dead end. The individual striving is the impetus of evolution, but it is the group that is the milieu which allows evolution to occur. Without the group the individual withers away.

The most fundamental,
the most significant,
the most intimate,
the most powerful
form of human relationship-
originating in the replication of matter at the dawn of time
-physical, chemical, genetic, biological, psychological, and social-
is parent-child.

iteration

Until the human being evolved, the mechanisms of survival were determined by genetically programmed response. The explosive growth of the human brain superseded the strictly glandular mechanisms and our survival is now determined by thought.

Consciousness is one dimension greater than replication, two dimensions greater than the matter/energy interaction in space/time.

the physical material of the universe created by the big bang
life on Earth engineered by replicators
the society of man determined by thought

The survival needs of human life are built into the organism and the mechanism for meeting those needs is culture- the function of our common mind. The evolution of the universe from lower and simpler to ever higher forms of coherence and complexity, from stable structures to reproductive life forms, has evolved from physical reaction to chemical reaction to biological reaction and now resides in psychological reaction. Human evolution - cultural transmission - occurs not only over generations, but in the life of each individual.

REPLICATION II

the reproductive act
the foundation for family
the fundamental unit of society
the inextricable bonding of individuals
conception and fetal development
absolute dependency
birth
and the biological drive for security

75% of the growth of the human brain occurs after birth. The structure of the brain cells neural firing patterns are determined by childhood experience. The most rapid and radical changes a person experiences are during her first two years of life.

We are genetically determined to seek security and it is mother to whom we look first. An infant is acutely sensitive to her environment, even to the extent of sensing the emotional climate around her. Infants seek experience and strive to understand and control their world, to solve problems and derive satisfaction from success.

The mother - infant relationship is the most significant determinant of the psychological and social development of the baby human. Food and physical maintenance are not enough to sustain human life.

The baby requires a sense of profound security through intimate, emotionally positive communication and concerned, caring physical contact - or more precisely - Love. Without that a baby will sicken and die or at best develop into an anti-social person who will require a hospital or prison.

Of course the mother - infant relationship is not the whole of human development, but it's influence is such that only extraordinary circumstances may outweigh it.

The family is the basis of the tribe and the tribe is the basis of the nation. The same criteria for healthy growth applies : Love.

Human society, now, is diseased.

The Division of People
- glorified as tribe-
whether national, political, racial, religious,
economic, corporate, or geographic
Is the Foundation of War.

The parent programs the child with what the world, the physical, psychological, and cultural environment programmed the parent. This is the creation of man and society. The fresh human brain is geared to mimic, the infant human is engineered to simulate the behaviors of the parent. The infant brain is a sponge absorbing whole the human experience to which it is exposed. Whether kind or cruel, secure or fearful, the child is subject, in every way (physically, psychologically, and socially) to the parent's authority.

By the time the child is 5 years old she will have been formed more by the physical contact, facial expressions, voice tones, body language, and general demeanors and attitudes of the parent than by any overt demands, commands, or expectations of whatever expanded social structures she grows into. The early influences are life long determinates-she will fit right into society because society grows out of the same family/tribal phenomena.

The parent sets the stage, creates the skeletal structure of the individual's persona, based upon the tradition that programs the parent-the acceptance of authority and prejudice towards those outside the tribe, propelling forward the contradictory nature of competition and compassion that characterizes humanity.

The paradox is realized as the glorification of the tribe into nations, religions, and corporations where the individual gives over her life's energy to the tribe and the tribe competes ruthlessly for resources.

Interlude II

the spirit of god
universal intelligence
pulls the human being forward
manifesting semi-consciousness
evidenced by the evolution
of our aesthetic sense
into high technology
and the awareness of right and wrong
(tribal only- not yet absolute- ergo: only semi-conscious)

The height of moral authority was achieved in prehistory and codified by Moses as the ten commandments- when we are able to live that law individually and collectively, we will be fully conscious.

The primal physical being we are- animal- tribal and prejudicial- is tugging us down to the ground- planet Earth- threatening to swallow us up, consciousness and all.

The emotional elements of existence, love and fear (the matters of life and death), are two aspects of one whole- you can't create god without the devil.

BOOK THREE

The Evolution of Our Common Mind
the flowering of thought
replication peaking

10,000 years ago
tribal man goes to war.
He forms tribes into states
and states into nations.

The self has begun it's march across time,
until now
it stands over the Earth,
ax in hand,
poised to split the planet in two.

Its time to recognize the power we wield
and turn it to better use.

the power to mold men's minds
in childhood

by the time man achieved domestication of plant and animal
he had created god and beauty
and a sharp metal edge
combined with a psyche that pursues security
ruthlessly
in the name of the tribe
-prejudice-
are born structures of power
with the one
-father, god, king, master, government-
on top
supported by the many
-children, mortals, subjects, slaves, citizens-
on bottom

Not much has changed since then... except for the sharp metal edge has become a sharp mental edge (legal) and vast machine capable of anything (technology) which, like a sharp metal edge, can do only a limited amount of good, depending on the quality of consciousness that wields it, swords, plowshares, computers, et al.

With the advent of the agricultural revolution, man achieved a high degree of success in his pursuit of security through knowledge, technique, and culture. He created the conditions for permanent communities, expanded populations, divisions of labor, distinctions of rank and privilege, and military capability for unifying disparate tribes, engaging enemies, plundering, taking slaves, and enforcing law.

Simple survival was no longer the total time and energy consuming goal of the whole community. The psyches of the more talented individuals were cultivated to create security through knowledge while the more privileged were given free reign to exploit power.

And the psyche of the laborer, foot soldier, and slave was squashed, molded, manipulated, and discarded- right along with his body.

The universal mind guided it all up to the point where the "particular" mind took over- the self- tribal individuals- me- culture, knowledge, technique, program, and prejudice- creating the present global chaos.

Atom Smashing! Earth Shattering!

HUMAN BEINGS ARE THE BUILDING BLOCKS
THOUGHT USES
TO PERPETUATE ITSELF

THE SAME WAY DNA USES AMINO ACIDS AND NUCLEOTIDES-
IT BUILDS STRUCTURES WHICH COMPETE

Mind Blowing!

Its kinda like sayin' everything you've ever thought about- your hopes, your dreams, your fears, your most cherished possessions, desires, activities, and memories, beautiful and horrible alike, your traditions and beliefs, the whole of your past- don't mean a whole heckuva lot to the universal mind, the spirit of god.

"You" and "me" and every thought we think is just an extension of the cosmic physical/chemical/biological/psychological reaction initiated by the big bang. There is no freedom in this.

what the universal mind is interested in is
the world/experience/consciousness/perception
that you're plugged into right here and now
remember?
this is it

Thought is great for maximizing physical security and comfort but that security and comfort is lost when thought attempts to do what it simply cannot do- cheat death.

At the dawn of civilization the initial insights have blossomed into advanced language, writing, mathematics, science, philosophy, religion, agriculture, engineering, navigation, law and every form of art. Only 5000 years ago, Adam, having swallowed the fruit, sees his nakedness and vulnerability builds walled cities, granaries, and armies and from out on the frontier he mounts a multitude of horses to consolidate the countryside through terror- violence- and he proliferates.

Certain structures of thought (the ones that promote the survival of the individual and foster pleasure) tend to dominate the environment of our common mind (human brain cells).

And so it came to pass that self, chief, and tribe should evolve into god, king, and country.

REPLICATION III

Through replication- DNA- life evolves.
Thought is an elastic, flexible, sometimes fluid form of replicator
existing in the primordial soup of human brain cells,
our common mind.
It's components consist of
memory, images, ideas, paradigms, and presuppositions.
It's structure is formed by
hopes, fears, desires, and dreams.
Thought uses human beings to perpetuate itself
through culture, custom, tradition, imitation, belief, prejudice, and
program,
institutions and organizations,
schools and government,
armies and war-
violence-
sanctioned by law.

Though now, through technology, its doing it's best to create silicon
and steel structures- machines and computers not subject to the biological
law of death- in order to conquer and control completely

GENESIS

out of Africa
the garden of Eden
man erupted
engulfing the globe
cultivating and civilizing
the Middle East, Egypt, India, and Asia

human social structures
are human entities
the characteristics of the individual human
are the characteristics of
human social structures

the history of the world
is the story of man
having risen from the bowels of the Earth
exploding outwardly

the history of mankind
is the story of human social structures
dividing the Earth's resources
through violence
and prominent personalities

social organizations in competition evolving
the stronger more powerful
devouring the weak naturally
by their ability to achieve security
through violence and technology
the primal motivation and means of the self

The abundance of wealth generated by knowledge and technique initiated the stratification of society while technology tended to solidify it's structure- man becoming dependent upon advanced techniques, ever necessitating further development to cope with the new conditions created by the original inventions- the exponential rate of population growth and the destruction of the natural environment being the primary consequence.

survival success
through thought
allows the animal within us
every excess of
exploitation, manipulation, and organization

Stone Age
50,000 years ago
bands of 20 to 30 people
hunting and gathering

25,000 years ago
tribes of 150 to 200 people
accessed archetypal insights
logical: numbers, calendars, maps
aesthetic: clothes, jewelry, painting, carvings
technical: spear launcher, bow and arrow

10,000 years ago
villages along river banks and in mountain valleys
agricultural revolution
pottery, weaving, wheels, plow, carts

7,000 years ago
metal

5,000 years ago
crop surpluses, population growth, cities
gods and kings
distinctions of rank and privilege
organized government
extensive irrigation systems, roads, and pyramids
written language, Hammurabi's code
specialization and division of labor
trade, money
music, paintings, sculpture
and war
-property-
****

a multifaceted, pulsating, sense oriented organism extends itself
the limit of it's senses
-territory-

the more highly evolved the sensory apparatus, the further the limit

all within that boundary is an aspect of itself

an ameba's boundary extends not much further than its cell wall

a human being's boundary by comparison is cosmic
-from stargazer to star flight-

34

Out of the most intense and intimate of human experiences- the whole human act of the biological cycle of reproduction- conception, birth, dependency, protection, nurturing, maturity, and conception etc.- survival- utterly animal, territorial, and tribal- *was born the concept of property.*

the providence of insight

the universe sprouts human beings
an extended family
they look around at the world
at the Earth and sky
and each other
and they know
in their blood
and in their soul
that they are connected

It is this connection that determines their behavior- the best assurance of survival is total and absolute investment in the protection and nurturing of one's family- love- a vital essence of life, to survive and reproduce, the primal passion.
Then they look over and see another extended family.

Human encounters,
whether spontaneous or engineered,
varied among countless situations
and consequences were determined by
genetic and cultural traits,
the degree of technology possessed,
and the specific geographical characteristics-
rivers, mountains, oceans,
deserts, jungles, forests,
and the natural environment of
wildlife, plant and animal,
and the abundance of resources
or the lack thereof.

Human relationship is war or peace according to whether one lives by violence born of ruthless selfishness, survival, animal instinct, and the glorification of the self or compassion born of the familial instinct of love, sharing and caring, sacrifice of self, and an awareness of the wholeness of life or a particular imbalance thereof.

either way, so far, in this world
technique, skill, knowledge, material resources,
and the concept of property
has allowed the more brutal to dominate through the sacrifice of others
for the perpetuation of self
-property-
like a mother protecting her young, or prehistoric man protecting his
hunting ground,
or the tribe protecting it's territory
-property-
is determined and maintained by power
the violence of technology

The folks who had spear throwers, bows and arrows, swords, the most skillful hunt organizers, horses and the ability to ride, boats and navigational skills, stores of grain, high walls, and the most ruthless individuals were the folks who gained and lost property according to who possessed, at any given time, the most advanced techniques and the most ambitious leaders (human history).

The willingness (or rather the keen desire) and ability to kill both animals and men is built into our brain, muscle, blood, and bone. If it weren't we wouldn't be here now. To be hungry and successfully hunt and kill an animal, clean, cook, and eat it provides a deep satisfaction to the single most overwhelming need man experiences. Imagine what level of gratification, both physical and psychological, you might achieve if you made war, were victorious in battle, and gained not only a days meal, but land, crops, stores, animals, and slaves to do your grudge work to insure your survival for an indefinite period of time- until a superior force came along.

The tribe would no longer be the most successful form of social organization. What became more successful were tribal alliances, kingdoms, states, and nations motivated and maintained by force and dependency on technology and environmental resources.

the culture of violence

The surplus of time, energy, and material provided by the early technologies allowed individuals who were more self centered to prosper and organize society around themselves through violence both subtle and gross. Industrious labor, wisdom, generosity, compassion, and any other example of virtue is easily overcome by the more physically powerful. Loud boastful talk, cunning, greed, and ruthlessness influences more extensively and gains material reward faster for oneself at the expense of others because of fear- conscious displays of violence communicates deeper within our brain and farther faster through our common mind than does the exposition of intelligence.

Violent individuals, the physically strong and most ruthless and selfish, begin to survive with the most success. They gain another dimension of power through fear. To fully exploit the power of fear, violence of every form, physical and emotional, had to be displayed in such a way to engrave it deeply within our mind. The grossest, most blatant displays of violence, especially those with no apparent reason or purpose, would be the most feared, as it would imply the threat of pain upon anyone at anytime with no way to prepare.

This is the origin of marauding hordes, pillage, rape, plunder, torture, and cruel and unusual punishment in the guise of divine right, manifest destiny, eminent domain, spreading the word of god, providing security and defense, and the dispensation of justice, service, and protection. Fear and violence became the ordering principles of society. The most ruthlessly selfish individuals structured society through military might with themselves in the top power positions, while the best warriors, the traders of goods, the craftsmen and artisans, and priests who could curry the favor of the gods enjoyed various degrees of privilege- while the common laborers, foot soldiers, and slaves performed their back breaking word and enjoyed no privilege or worse.

You only know your social status in relation to others- there is no difference between glorifying yourself and demeaning others- violence is the fundamental nature of the self in society because the self is born of fear.

the evolution of our common mind
reiterated

thought
as a replicator
had come to control
the world
by dominating man's psychic energy
and the whole activity of humanity on Earth
is in the service of the self

the self of our common mind
-fragmented-
controls the world
-divided-
creating conflict
-inherent-

the process of thought
planted in our brain
by our parents
-authority, the tribe, society, et al-
at the dawn of human history
has manifest
as an accelerating
rapidly expanding
state of deterioration
of human relationship
and of the environment
approaching critical mass

The core paradigm of human thought is the self/god polarity. The cognizance of pattern and progression, of beauty, quality, and goodness, and the ability to reach out, put hands on, and acquire more abundant life through the function of brain cells, the whole of thought, technology and culture- this is man, potential god- as the first replicator was potential human through the test and trial of evolution. *We are now at the sub-primitive "dinosaur" stage of our psychic evolution.*

The original archetypes imposed themselves on the human brain through the imperative of communication- our common mind. Perception was symbolized by sound and gesture- language- simulated in the brain cells with the components of memory- and here man became caught in time with terrible results. Because man confused the *symbol* - images and ideas, the whole of thought- with *reality*. As if the self were the whole show, rather than what it is, a convention of language. It wasn't the self that germinated the seed of insight which sprouted the process of culture that civilized man. It wasn't the self that created biological entities capable of insight. The initial insights were a direct result of the universal mind probing our common space/time continuum via the human brain. Through the innocent, untouched, emerging mind of man- our common mind- the initial insights occurred to disparate people all over the globe at about the same time. That was the garden of Eden, when the function of the human brain was aligned with the workings of the cosmos- the universal mind- as was the whole of life which grew out of the planet. Insight was the result of pure, direct human perception. That perception was reflected in thought, simulated, analyzed, organized, and manipulated in harmony with the whole, producing more abundant life.

all these
and every other process of thought
arises out of the observation of memory

the moment you have more than one memory
the comparison begins
to measure each perception
with what is known
to judge emotionally
according to pleasure and pain

invariably eliciting an action
which is inevitably selfish

as the human brain produced technical miracles in the world
-power-
controlling the forces of nature
fire (protection, warmth, cooking)
water (fishing, irrigation, travel)
wind (sailing)
stars (navigation)
Earth (agriculture, material)
-through thought-
the evolution of culture
each generation taking for granted the miracles of the previous generation
producing ever greater degrees of gratification through technology
thought came to consume all the psychic energy available

as thought evolved
creating superior survival skills
simulating the world in the brain

40

it was only one step removed
from reflecting itself
as a part of the whole process
apart from the whole process

when it did
the self was born
and became a replicating entity
in and of it's own
-with a different priority than that of the whole organism-

the primary priority of the whole human being who is fully aware of her
intimate and intense human and environmental relationships
is the well being of her loved ones

the only priority of the self
is it's own survival
-"me"-

the curse/blessing polarity

by usurping the control of behavior
from the purely animal
-out of which we were born-
thought
-the self-
multiplied exponentially
our ability to survive
pursue pleasure and avoid pain

by allowing the self
-me-
to determine our behavior
to govern our lives
we lose contact
with the universal mind
-intelligence-
god
takes the role of object
-thing-
subject to the action of the self

Which conjures up that old traditional character- Lucifer- the devil- in
the role of "the self"- born of the fear of death. So come to find out, god
did create the devil, as a tool of evolution- a spark, a tension- a spur to
creation, but only as a bit player in a minor role who stole the scene but
aint the whole show.

The Rant of Syndax Vuzz

BOOK FOUR

GOD PROPERTY AND THE STRUCTURE OF THOUGHT

500 years ago

catholic church
circumnavigation of planet
magna carta
patent law
mathematics
printing press
dissection of human body
telescope and microscope
gun powder
cannon

250 years ago

collapse of monarchies
masthusian/machiavellian politics
descarte's philosophy
newton's laws
industrial revolution
democracy, socialism, communism
declaration of independence
united states constitution
declaration of rights of man and citizen
vaccinations
steam engines

100 years ago

alleged freedom of slaves and women
world war one
Einstein
human flight
atomic theory
genetics
internal combustion engine
automobile
radio
telephone
electric motor
camera
cocaine
cell theory
mass production
ball bearing
skyscraper
refrigerator
machine gun

75 years ago

quantum mechanics
cinema
television
Godel's theorem
penicillin
empire state building
atom smasher
liquid fuel rocket

50 years ago

the united nations
declaration of human rights
DNA identified
mass consumption
open heart surgery
computers
satellites in space
laser
world war two
jet air plane
atomic bomb

25 years ago

global democratic/communist conflict
man goes to moon and back
human heart transplant
DNA mapped
test tube babies
personal computers
LSD
space station
robots

NOW

what's goin' on
&
what it is

or

the pit of human behavior
&
the pinnacle of perception

or

how the head
-out of fear-
forces the hands
to cut the throat
of our common being
-while god watches-

the mass media, most notably television, and our personal and public
technological communications systems, local and global
PLUS
capitalism- the acquisition and distribution system of our planetary
resources- established by
the self through slavery
PLUS
our polluted environment
PLUS
all of us together, the whole of human relationship
EQUALS
a primitive planetary being

an electronic nervous system
an economic circulatory system
an ailing respiratory system

and a twisting, churning digestive system
-that's the poor being poisoned-

That is our self in common,
a primitive, stone-age consciousness
with space-age tools,
an immense power controlled
by a small fragmented mind,
our common mind.

The Poverty of the Planet

The foundation of our present worldwide social structure
is a mass of rotting, stinking corpses
upon which sit starving children with bloated bellies
whose despairing mothers
are parchment wrapped skeletons,
while teenage boys with guns
shoot indiscriminately at the innocent and guilty alike
to instill fear
and prove a warped manhood
in search of a petty glory.

Then there are the soldiers
in the hills outside the city
and in the trenches
and in the cover of burned out urban dwellings
and the rubble of once thriving market places,
where again innocent citizens die
as the result of a mistaken service.

There are also those few regions of relative stability with varying degrees of prosperity, from the poor and destitute of the vast slums to the affluence of those with property. As the power of technology and the scope of authority increases, the health and stability of the people decreases. Our global social condition is epitomized in our cities, while the destructive, deteriorating human behavior in the cities is epitomized by the psyche of the individual.

Thanks to high technology decreasing the death rate and increasing the birth rate and releasing the vast majority from having to work the farm, the over population of the world gravitates toward the pit- the great urban centers where they spend their lives conspicuously making, buying, selling, using, and disposing of things. That is, if they are of the more fortunate whose numbers are dwindling. If not- as a result of the biological laws of over crowding (savage competition, increased physical and mental disease, sexual perversion, the breakdown of the family, pervasive violence both subtle and gross) then they are of a proportion of the people whose numbers are exploding even faster than is the population as a whole- the poor and destitute, the criminal, the violent, and the insane.

Due to our need to compensate psychologically for the expanding fear and tension and the ill health that we must deal with daily, we begin to shift the parameters of what is considered "normal" to include what was once deviant, which in turn contributes further to our moral decline. An effect snowballing synergistically with the destruction of our environment and the wasting of our resources brought about by the conspicuous making, buying, selling, using, and disposing of things on a global scale.

Its that inherently contradictory nature of ourselves
-cooperative/competitive-
where we give over our life
to the religion, nation, corporation,
or whatever organization,
(usually the power structure we were born into)
and these organizations compete ruthlessly for resources
in a world exploding with ever more powerful social structures.

which evolved out of the tendency of the universe
to form ever higher and more complex forms of organization

in circles and cycles
and spheres of influence
expanding and contracting

subatomic, atomic, molecular
biological, psychological, social
local, global, and cosmic

The social organization of the world is rooted in the structure of thought,
the structure which dominates the world of man,
the structure whose foundation is culture, the creator of our civilization.

the self is the center
with god
as motivation and justification
to conquer and control
to gain property
to finance technique
to conquer
to gain property
with god
as motivation and justification
ad infinitum, as nauseum

A Cancerous Anarchy

cancer- potentially unlimited growth
anarchy- absence of order- without government

The most powerful social structures on Earth are international corporations backed by the most powerful governments on the planet. Their goals and objectives are as old as man himself yet never before has there been so extensive and unstoppable power and influence in the world thanks to the physical size of the world's population and the explosion of technology. With assets that exceed the gross national products of most nations, they virtually control the world's laws or at the very least sidestep them. There is no international body to govern these giants.

Slick, blood and grease covered floors, flashing razor sharp knives, saws and giant meat grinders of the slaughter house, dust and gas filled air of the mines, fatally toxic and highly combustible chemicals of the refineries, the radiation of the nuclear power and weapons industries- these are only a few examples of the multitude of conditions under which people risk their lives, health, and the well being of their families for the sake of owners, executives, managers, stockholders, and customers of gargantuan, faceless, inhuman corporations. Protected by the laws, police, and military forces of governments effectively bought and controlled, the captains, stockholders, and stewards of these corporations have, apparently, nothing to lose and every immoral, material luxury to gain, all at the expense of their laborers and consumers blood, sweat, and tears. Not only are our individual lives, but the health of the whole planet has been compromised and in many cased damaged, at least to the extent of several human generations to come.

International corporations possess a positive potential, yet as of the present time, they are like a malignant cancer spreading throughout the body of mankind. Through their colossal advertising budgets and their experts of unethical enticement, hypnotism, and illusion, this cancer has engulfed the brain stem of our global society and is taking over the brain as a whole- the human brain- the common mind we all share- the thoughts and images which determine our behavior, individual and collective. Our government, our educational system, and our academic research are all controlled by or at least steered toward the goal of big business- the perpetuation of profit and the expansion of the organization.

Of course for every harmful situation these monsters create, there are actions that would redeem and correct- if they would just consider what is right for the people and planet rather than just what will profit and expand. The technology for controlling pollution is available yet not fully developed and implemented because it does not produce immediate, tangible profit. The technology for harnessing the absolutely unlimited energy of the only nuclear reactor, god given, this solar system needs- the sun- is a hair's breadth away, and will remain so until the energy corporations figure out how to put a meter between you and the sun.

And who foots the bills for these international, immoral madhouses to live, grow, thrive, and destroy? You and I, the little guys are the vast majority who produce, pay for and consume the marginally useful, often times hazardous to your health, sanity, and environment goods and services pushed at us with images of healthy, young, beautiful, financially fit, laughing, singing, dancing, smoking, drinking people in opulent surroundings on television, billboards, magazines, and movies.

Our circulatory system, the economy, is so clogged by these cancers we find survival to be at best meaningless and oftentimes a nightmare when we find so little of reality matches the false images that are set up to be our standard of living. We produce with our life's blood the labor that actually feeds the corporation. But little or nothing comes back. The circulation is cut off. We are losing our blood and getting duller and weaker by the minute, unaware of what health is, much less acquiring cure for our disease. All the while we are dependent upon the greedy destructors of our planet.

In the united states, 10% of the people own 73% of all wealth, while the other 90% of the people own only 27% of the wealth. Yet the laborers in the u.s. live like kings compared to nearly everyone in the third world, where tens of thousands of children die *each day* of malnutrition, disease, poverty, and neglect. The annual income of the poorest two and a half *billion* people on the planet equals the combined wealth of the world's richest *225* people. 20% of the global population receives approximately 80% of the world's income, while 80% of the people share the other 20% of the wealth. The poor folks in the rich countries are taxed to provide the rich folks in the poor countries "foreign aid for economic and technological development" so that the international corporations can fatten their bellies at the expense of the labor and resources of the undeveloped nations where medicine, food, and consumer products banned in the u.s. are dumped indiscriminately on unsuspecting consumers. What is it? Divine Right, Manifest Destiny, or Eminent Domain? You tell me, 'cause I wanna know.

With the population exploding at the rate it is, too many people may be the single greatest threat we face. The world population has more than tripled since the turn of the century. With over five billion people on Earth now, those who study population growth believe there will be over eight billion in fifty years. Yet it is not the number of people who place stress on the planet so much as the behavior in which they indulge. A baby born in Kenya will not grow up to drive cars, use air conditioners and refrigerators or eat grain feed beef. It will not grow up wasting non-renewable resources nor using huge amounts of energy. The activities in which it partakes will not contribute to undermining the life-support capabilities of the planet. We in the united states and the lifestyles we teach our children are, in fact, directly responsible for the greatest part of the destruction of the world. One rich person in the u.s., by investing in corrupt corporations, destroys more rain forest than a poor person trying to survive in the forest itself.

Its not that there is a lack of wealth, but that its not being distributed equitably. The technology and resources are available to provide more than enough life support for every being of the planet, but they are not being exploited to their greatest potential. If they were, present intelligence indicates the world population would stabilize. The present structures of power, the great religious organizations, the national governments, and the international corporations will not bring about the radical changes the present crisis demands because doing so would imply their demise.

The sad fact is that they are capable and willing to fight to the death- survive at any cost.

The Global War Machine

Ten percent of the planet's economy is in the production and service of war. Vast amounts of money, billions of dollars every day, gathered through taxes and spent as defense contracts, fuels the war machine and feeds the capitalist economy which weds big business and government whose offspring are over a hundred million strong, globally.

They are soldiers, police, and every type of weapons maker- laborer, scientist, engineer, and doctor making every kind of weapon, from clubs and shields, mace and armor, to computers, satellites, and intercontinental ballistic missiles armed with nuclear warheads of chemically or biologically lethal agents.

It takes over a hundred million people, globally, to keep the machine up and runnin'- part of the sum of people swelling the ranks of the paranoid and alienated who bring new meaning to what was once considered "normal", "rational", and "respectable". It may or may not be twisted logic that has brought the world to the point where security means the ability to annihilate the whole of human civilization in half an hour- but one thing's for sure- its accepted by all, but a very few.

In an insane world, insanity becomes the norm.

structures of power
forming and transforming
outwardly
joining
the fearful and greedy
the clever and cruel
the stupid and brutish
overcoming
the industrious and meek
the lovers of family and community
the open, honest, innocent, and true
dividing humanity
nationally, religiously, politically, economically
growing
larger, more complicated, impersonal, and inhumane
ever more far reaching
unwieldy, entrenched
powerful beyond control
fragmented and unwhole
creating
enmity and hatred
and their own opposition

whether they be
men on horseback with spears
against men on foot with clubs
or vast armies led by
khans, alexanders, napoleons, or hitlers
or protestant against catholic in Ireland
or jew against Palestinian in Israel
or christian against muslim in Beirut
or shiite against sunni in Saudi Arabia
or hindu against muslim in India
or black against afrikaaner in South Africa
or Iraqi vs. Kurd or Iran vs. Iraq
or Lebanon vs. Israel or Vietnam vs. Cambodia
or serb vs. croat or terrorist vs. innocent
or white against black in america
or crip vs. blood or rich vs. poor
or liberal vs. conservative or labor vs. management
or believers vs. non-believers or us against them

Structures of power are creating a magnitude of violence we, the people,
cannot endure.

power
authority, control, influence, strength
structure
something arranged in a definite pattern of organization

The structure of power is an essential facet of evolution. It makes matter. Atoms bond, form molecules which bond in their turn and form compounds. That's stability. Power structures are a natural tool of evolution. A collective action is taken to ensure the continuation of life.

A cell, complete in itself, joins other cells to form a more complex organism, more capable of thriving in it's environment than the cell is by itself. The more complex organisms band together in increasing complexity in order to survive, expand, grow, explore and reproduce until life evolves into man.

Human structures of power originate as a natural outcome of human survival. Man lives in groups. The animal instinct causes division according to perceived differences between groups and competition for resources. What binds individuals to act as a whole- kin, community, tradition, belief, climate, culture, etc., is exactly what divides a particular power structure from all others. As long as their is division there is conflict.

A structure of power is not just a collection of folks bonded by certain characteristics, but a specific form of organization in which each individual has a particular role. Life assigns us, each person, our role according to the place and time of our birth, our ancestors genes, our parents, our environment, our cultures. We learn to play our part at an early age and our whole life is spent maintaining our structures inwardly, as our program or belief system and outwardly as our society. Whether we grow from girl scout into politician or school yard bully into policeman or video game champ into white collar criminal or confused kid into laborer, we are all doing our part to maintain the present global social order.

We derive tremendous emotional security in knowing our roles well and diligently playing our part because our programming works automatically, like a machine. We don't have to face the unknown, or take responsibility for our thought, feelings, and behavior.

The more coherent the structure is, the greater the forces that act on the individual. The more sharply defined the position is, the less freedom exists. Although, from time to time, certain individuals may change position, high or low, within the structure, the positions always remain the same. Only the faces change.

A structure of power has a life of it's own that functions strictly beyond the capacity of any one particular person. Many individuals may die, but the structure of power just keeps rollin' along, from generation to generation. The structure of power becomes more important than living people, prejudicial ideas and tyrannical leadership thrives. If an individual's or group's existence impedes or merely does not enhance a greater power, then the lesser power must be ignored, absorbed, or destroyed- through political oppression, corporate acquisition, the "criminal justice system," or war.

Meanwhile our knowledge and power steadily increases, allowing our animal instincts and human emotion to be an ever increasing force in the world. This force dominates the natural environment and governs our planetary society and determines every aspect of human relationship.

When we see that all humanity shares a common bond more powerful than any belief, location, nation, or religion - more significant than any tradition or family name - when we see that we share a common mind, the human brain, we will create a structure of power, a one world super structure, in which power is diffused through a network rather than administered by a bureaucracy.

Ruthless Selfishness Revisited

its out on the frontier
where evolution makes it's breaks
where small segments of the population
-stressed beyond the normal limits of survival-
will gradually die off
or
suddenly transform

should the transformation be
sufficiently radical
the minority may, in turn, transform the whole

after a hundred thousand years of tribal existence in essential equilibrium
the past ten thousand years has spawned and evolved human organizations
that have grown and spread over the whole planet
in quantum leaps and exponential proportions

while what was one common to all
-Earth-
became property
that has changed hands
through violence
from one empire to another

until now
in less than one century
the ruler
a mutant
the united states of america
with a stranglehold on the vast majority
doesn't realize
its about to be grabbed by the balls

yeah
wars and slavery
rape, pillage, and plunder
that's the fuel of the fire
that ignited civilization
through the spark of culture
that's now burning up the world

While the tribes gathered, cooperated, worshipped the goddess, and cultivated the lands in the river valleys, the nomads were roaming the steppes on horses. At the edge of existence, they worshipped the gods of the mountains, of thunder and lightning. Where the farmers worshipped the goddess, the giver of life, the ability to cultivate and grow, the pastoralists worshipped the gods, the takers of life, the willingness to destroy and plunder. Peaceful, abundant coexistence characterized life in the garden of Eden. The slaughter of human beings and the pillaging of their property and the subjugation of the living- slavery- the glorification of the power and use of the sword epitomized the people on the periphery.

The tillers of the soil were egalitarian, there was compassion and care for the whole community. The nomads were concerned with the strict hierarchy, the strongest and most ruthless dominating all. As the nomads explored their power through death and destruction, inciting fear far and wide, their influence intruded into the core of a highly sophisticated humanity, thousands of years old, that lived in harmony with the whole amidst material abundance.

The power of the war gods was unmatched. The farmers had no natural inclination or skill or tools to deal with the marauders the only way they could have been dealt with successfully. There was nothing to stop the intruders from confiscating the land and the wealth and enslaving the people and creating the social order in which we now live.

Like a hot virus that moves in, takes over, and destroys it's host, the marauding hordes were able to do a lot with a little. And that little is called fear. It now controls our whole world. The ability to conquer and control is the most highly valued skill of our planetary society. Lying, scheming politicians, corporate executives, investors, gangs, and crooked cops rule our streets and our world.

But come to find out- the world can't by controlled. The greater the ability to control, the greater the potential for catastrophic changes to occur. The more pressure the greater the risk of explosion.

the establishment of human civilization
thousands of years ago
was the establishment of the social structure
in which we now live

thought has created great structures of power
every type of
nation, army, industry
international corporation and religious organization
-and the rich and powerful who finance and operate them-
and every type of alliance and rift
where always a few at the top exist
experiencing immense power and pleasure
ease, comfort, and fantastic physical security
and are supported by the many at the bottom
existing in degraded deprivation and pain
as receivers of the so called generosity
dispensed by those in power

That's thought's job- to seek ruthlessly to survive. But why, twenty
five years after thought has attained the knowledge necessary to supply
every human being of the planet with the maximum physical security
possible, do we still live in the squirming conglomeration of an anarchic
hierarchy of ruthlessly competing power structures?

SLAVERY

HELL INCARNATE
&
UTTERLY EVIL

Need We Enumerate Every Point of Pain?

Abduction
Rape
Torture
Murder

The Desolation of Families
&
The Disease of Generations

That Is Destroying Us Today

based upon the false concept of property
-culturally transmitted-
these thousands of years
practically hardwired into our brain
the common mind we all share

-ya know-
its that polar extreme again

remember?

The one can't exist without the other.

ya know what i mean?

I'm talkin' about
not puttin'
our responsibility
on
god and the devil
anymore.

NO MASTERS
&
NO SLAVES

SLAVE LABOR

It Built the World

From the Tower of Babel
To the Pyramids
To the Wall of China
To the Foundation of World Dominance
By the United States of America

Without slavery, europeans could not have created the system of capitalism that operates our world and human relationship. It required vast amounts of wealth, both actual and symbolic, to initiate and establish so successful a system of subjugation. While lots of folks like to point out newton's science and the philosophies of machievelli, malthus, and descartes as the means and motivation of the most recent phase of human evolution, they rarely mention that it was slave labor- the black african in particular, with some help from chinese and indian and native lands stolen- that was the force and raw material that created the planetary wealth that is enjoyed, in particular, by the white, christian, european, and american.

and its those same
white, christian
europeans and americans
that's runnin' things now

all based on that odd notion we call
property
(Death puts the concept of property in it's proper perspective.)
so absurd a notion
that it requires the point of a sword
to make it believable

but now the idea of property has taken root
in our psychological soil
-fertilized by the fear of death for thousands of years-
it has become nearly fossilized
impossible to cut down

but that's ok
we have merely to leave it alone
undisturbed
it will become a relic
a memento of our primitive past

60

The most common form of slavery today is debt bondage.
-actual for the poor and virtual for the rich-
The one is physical and the other mental.
each equally catastrophic

The poor are paid less than it takes to live a healthy life.
-ergo-
They are forever in debt.
'cause there's never enough money

The rich pursue a futile illusion of security.
-at the expense of the poor-
Because there is never enough money.
to buy off death

though they may not hold complete legal title
over our body, mind, and soul
the result is the same

ok! ok!
let's cut the crap
and stop beatin' about the bush
and call it what it is in today's world

-labor-

that's what it all boils down to
-labor/management-

the rest is just conflict
between the managements of power structures
in competition
for dividing the spoils

or

laborers
acting out their petty dramas
searching for glory
in the midst of poverty

the poor take the shit
so the rich don't hafta

its labor
that works the whole world
according to the plan
laid out by management

It is the laborer who makes possible our ability, or lack thereof, to carry out whatever activity we participate in. It is labor that produces our food, picks up the garbage, builds our homes, and buries our dead and carries out the essential every day tasks of mankind.

There is an innate nobility in those who labor. It is not just putting in a hard days work that makes a laborer, anyone may put in a days work, gain from it, and feel good about it. It is laborers who sacrifice their lives so that a few others may prosper. A laborer lives his or her life, day after day, year in and year out, at the bottom of society. He not only supports his dependents at subsistence level or worse, but sees his work create great wealth for those who stand over him directing his life's energy and determining the material quality of his life.

It is not the owners and managers of property, machinery, and materials, who create real, tangible wealth. They play only a small, abstract, secondary role that could be replaced with a clerk and a computer. It is the people who get up every day and go to jobs where they perform physical, repetitious, monotonous, mind numbing work that nobody would do for it's own sake that creates wealth. Let the workers stay home and see what gets done.

But the saddest part of it all is that the laborer, in order to perform the tasks society demands, in order for her and her family to survive, the laborer must kill off the most valuable part of herself, her true creativity, her freedom to see the potential for truth and beauty in the world and human relationship. Because if she does not kill off that part of herself, she will take immediate action to dismantle the corrupt, contaminated society in which she lives- and that might risk her ability to survive. Its the factor of fear built into our society. Hidden from humanity, its the linchpin that holds the absurdities together- the fear of death. Ignoring the fact of our death, the self rules society.

As long as we live under the conditions where the goal of the big wigs runnin' things is to obtain the greatest amount of work for the least amount of pay and the goal of the worker is to gain the most pay for the least work, there will be no lasting peace. For a time, in a few instances, there may be a truce, while the laborer's needs are sufficiently satisfied. While his mind is occupied with things like cars, televisions, telephones, and refrigerators, his belly full and his mind stupefied by various entertainments, there may be a period of superficial satisfaction for a segment of workers. But it cannot last. A slave well taken care of is still a slave.

Our material standards will never have a chance of matching our master's material standard. Because of the boss's power position, he will continue to move closer to his goals to the same extent we move further from ours. The gulf between the rich and the poor widens. There is a growing global consciousness of the gross injustice perpetrated by the powerful over the weak. The more we are aware of this, the more we will refuse to accept it.

The foundation of the global injustice that rules our world is the concept of property. Certain aspects of property arise obviously and naturally in life, while other aspects are imposed by military force, police, judges, and jails. The whole world is divided up- everything is owned by somebody. Some few of recognized property rights are actual, most are abstract. What is real is the food on your table, the clothes on your back, and the roof over your head. What is absurdly abstract is ownership of any fragment to the Earth.

Among equally provisioned persons, questions concerning and disputes over ownership rarely occur. Its in the presence of unequal wealth distribution- as it so grossly is in the world today- that the ownership of property is the central issue of human relationship. It is the absolutely absurd, abstract, and arbitrary aspect of our concept of property that makes in necessary to use weapons to prop it up. Property originated with military might and has been passed down to us today through a tradition of inheritance and wars between structures of power.

The concept of ownership, born with the self, the me, creating 'mine', as opposed to you and yours, the first splinter of fragmentation in the mind of man is an idea born of the fear that the thing one now holds may be lost. We so readily ignore death. Ownership is a social convention to maintain order within a group of people, a convention to be used or tossed aside at the whim of a holder of power. A convention to be used or tossed aside by a group of people dealing with another group, an excuse for war, exploitation, and brutality. The ownership of property is the major source of income for the minority who control the worlds wealth.

How does an owner derive profit from owning a factory, or any stockholder of any corporation for that matter? He doesn't actually hold the factory as a physical activity. He doesn't stick it in his pocket and take it to the store and pull dollar bills out of it. The owner does, however, possess an imaginary, though legal, type of control over the functioning of the business.

What actually produces the profit are people, the people who mass produce, mass market, and mass consume the world of products and services. The little people who survive on a minimal wage, who operate the machines in the factories, who go down in the mines, who build the buildings, who harvest the crops, who actually put their minds and bodies on the line daily, in back breaking labor, produce the profit for owners.

And buddy, you better believe that very little of that profit goes to improve the life of the laborer, much less anyone worse off. It is we who live in poverty who provide for the rich. We take the shit so the rich don't hafta. The reason is simply because we are stronger and more intelligent-intelligence being "the ability to deal with...trying situations". We have to be in order to survive. The rich don't do anything intelligent, they just use information and power to manipulate ideas, events, people, and material to maintain the status quo.

I've been a laborer living in poverty most of my life and I find it no wonder that the working man is so easily held down. He's worn out from working all the time to get a little further behind in the rat race. And of course he done been psychologically euthanatized at an early age. Then he spends the rest of his life struggling with those who control power and their minions.

Though the validity of this imaginary legal concept of ownership usually lies in some desk drawer, safety deposit box, or an obscure file cabinet or shelf in some distant government building, it is seemingly more concrete and more significant than the actual "ownership" a man possesses of his own life. The laborer owns his life if nothing else, yet he is forced to turn around and sell himself daily for an hourly wage- essentially nothing in relation to his true worth- and participate in an activity which produces profit for someone who doesn't actually need it.

In far too many cases, the very goods and services provided by laborers for the company are themselves destructive to the planetary well being, for instance- the love canal, three mile island, or that chemical company atrocity in bhopal. Then, when the affected folks look for assistance from the authorities responsible, come to find out, nobody gives a damn. Responsibility is shifted to that fictitious legal entity, the corporation. The corporation takes the blame while the owner vacations at the beach.

Ownership is the dust in the wind of human affairs. It comes and goes at the whim of fate. There is no lasting reality behind the concept of ownership. I now have to admit that it doesn't make sense to say I own my life or my body or even my perception. Because there is no "I" separate from these that could be said to hold or possess them. Although most of us live our lives as if there were a separate self in possession or control.

who owns your life?
by what authority do you exist?
the state?
the corporation?
your mate?
yourself?
who owns what?

Its all too ephemeral and relative.

Ownership is a social convention manipulated by those who hold power.
It has no independent reality other than conceptual.

-in actuality-
in the light of death
what could ownership possibly mean?

That ownership that human beings are able to pull off is only for a short time anyway and property is central to the division of the planet and human relationship. There is no division without conflict.

PROPERTY
-money-
DETERMINES OUR BOUNDARIES
-conflicts-
AND OUR HUMAN RELATIONS
-violent-

The single most direct and accurate measurement of power through property in the world today is one step further into abstraction to that symbol of wealth we most often refer to as money. This ancient abstract symbol has more substance in our corrupt global culture than all the starving people in india and africa combined. We live in a world whose greatest determinant of human relationship is a man made symbol of wealth which in itself has no practical human value, as actual food, clothing, and shelter. The only value intrinsic to money is as an intellectual and legal construct stored in a vault downtown or as information in cyberspace. This creation of man's mind, this imagination, backed by law- police, judges, and jails- determines not only the quality of our material life but also our personal and collective interactions. The quality and location of our housing, our educational opportunities and facilities, our food, clothing, and health care, our political power and our legal rights, in fact, how we meet all our needs is determined by whatever particular amount of money we have access to. Keep in mind all this occurs in a system created by selfish, fearful minds and enforced by violence. Its not just happening in particular places at this point in history, its the whole world and it originated long ago and that's probably why we don't question it. Its not a matter of the truth of one or another belief or opinion or theory of what is happening. Its a matter of what's right and what's wrong. Its not a matter of who has the power to fool people through conditioning by seductive images or who has the power and inclination to force people through threats, fear, and violence into certain modes of thought and behavior. Because the fact of what's right will be all that's left after the inevitable destruction of what is wrong occurs. What's wrong is what is runnin' the world now. What concerns us here and now is, will it crumble from within, destroying us all as the natural result of our ignoring 'what is', or will we step back and look at the whole of life and make a conscious collective decision to create a new world.

THE MATTER OF INTELLIGENCE

-a fact demanding recognition-

Who is, actually, the most intelligent?

-intelligence-
the ability to learn or understand
or to deal with new or trying situations

a mind divided within itself is schizoid at best
and our common mind is divided countless ways
-racially, nationally, politically, religiously, economically, socially,
ideologically-
(the whole of culture in all it's aspects and influences)
but the most potent division is sexual

in order for any system of rank to be maintained
it is vital that the feminine half of humanity be suppressed
the half whose genetic and biological imperative
is loving and caring
and practical, devoted, daily activity
the subjugation of the female
is and always has been
attained by physical and material force
-same as all evil is accomplished-

the next most potent division is racial

when I look into a black face
I see the strength and the grace
that has endured
the desolation of generations

when I look into a white face
I see the fear of a lost soul
seeking ruthlessly
his own personal security

It is certainly not my intent to encourage any type of racism, bigotry,
or prejudice- but until we look the facts in the face and deal directly with
them, they'll keep poppin' up, interfering with whatever we may want to
create.

I was lucky enough the other day to have a pleasant conversation with one good ol' boy with whom I had been acquainted a number of years. How our conversation made it's way 'round to a particular social phenomena, I can't recall. We were talkin' 'bout the urban poor of the united states of america- of which, I am one. He asked me a question that went somethin' like this, in reference to the unfortunate, "Are they stupid, lazy, ignorant, or what?". At that point I had an almost overwhelming desire to take that question in my fist and deposit it, through his esophagus, into his small intestines. Fortunately, for both our sake, I was able toward off the temptation. Instead, I calmly posed him a hypothetical scenario: your forefathers, rather than being the abductors they were, instead were abducted themselves from a faraway paradise, transported on slave ships and had endured lifetimes of torture, abuse, and inhumane treatment generation after generation for hundreds of years until now, one generation after major federal legislation had granted a few basic human rights that still aren't fully recognized in the day to day affairs of your society, making for a deprived, humorless existence and a bleak future- might not you behave in ways that would appear destructive to the corrupt society in which you found yourself?

And I Say
If You Did Not
Then You Would Be
Either
A Saint
Or
A Spineless Worm

HEY!
ya know
what I'm fixin' ta tell ya
makes me feel
kinda
...well...
I don't know
-sick-
I guess

'cause
...well...
its like revealin'
a deep secret of shame
-not one I been keepin' in my closet-
but one I seen in yours

What makes me sick is that I see you forgot its there. Now don't get me wrong. I understand. If I had that in my closet, I'd spend lifetimes through generations denying it or blaming you for it, too- **but I aint the one.**

so
even though
I see
you think
you're ok with me
and I don't want to bust yo bubble
-really I do-

first
try this one on for size
you have no idea
the magnitude
of the god awful righteous hatred
that I
carry in my soul
for you
it would burn down yo house
with you and yo family
in it

and the fear
that my woman feels
for the health and safety and future
of her children

-yeah-
I know
ya wanna blame me
ya think
ya god
or somethin'
but
only god
creates a world
of humans
then steps back
and judges them
according to the decisions they make
regardless of the circumstances
over which they have no control
then rewards them
with heaven or hell

or is that just a god you made up
to try and trick me
-whatever-
I don't give a damn!
yeah
you know it
-hell-
I'll tell ya this here too
-yeah-
you created me
I'm sorry that sticks in yo craw
-not!-
ya brought me here
through my ancestors
who ya brutalized
beyond
the point of human recognition
and we survived
and endured
unto a strength
beyond your comprehension
we have survived whole
as a good and decent people
who want only
the same as you
-we deserve more-

-yeah-
there's a growing number of us
who are actually beginning
to absolutely refuse
to accept the injustice
any longer
-in the street, schools, jobs, business, and government-
-fuck it-
as the truth becomes
more public knowledge
a critical mass will be achieved
and there's gonna be
an ear piercing
metallic scream
and a great grinding of gears
and the machine
of a corrupt society
gonna come to a screechin' halt

-yeah-
you created me
with your global order
-vietnam, kuwait, panama, somalia-
you pumped me up
with glorious images
of the godfather, dirty harry, rambo
and television all day long
ya taught me
how easy it is
to shoot a gun
-hell yeah-
I'm gonna cop an attitude
of fierce aggression
-back off muthafucka-
I'm gonna have
what society values
-fuck you-
I'm gonna have
cars, clothes, jewelry
electronic equipment
by whatever means necessary

ya aint gonna dis me
bitch
and ya think
I'm gonna
flip burgers
or stack boxes
or clean up yo yard
-I don't think so-
but if I do
come do any of that
or build yo cars
or roads
for a minute
don't think
I'm gonna
bust my ass
-'cause I aint-

maybe 50%
I figure
puttin' out
'bout 50%
about right
stay on the job
a few days
weeks
-whatever-
you can bust yo ass
if ya wanna
-I'll watch-
I don't see why
I should bust ass
just to make
some rich folks richer
and they just tear me off
a little bit
the smallest
they think
they can get away with

-nah-
you
go on ahead
I say
fuck the team
I aint
on yo team
that's
where
you're
put to the test
-whose side-
ya gonna take
?
team leader
supervisor
or
worker
laborer
-master-
or
-slave-
?

yeah that's right
you made me
so here I am
in yo face
you showed me
how to make some money
who my real friends are
how to gain respect
how to feel good about myself
and
how to organize
and fight to the death
for colors
whether they be
red, white, blue, or black
take yer pick
-we're out here doin' it-
we're the front line soldiers
wagin' a war
that's creepin' right on up to yo do' step
and ya act like ya don' even see it comin'

74

out on the inner urban frontier
the youth of today
are the heirs
to generations
and hundreds of years
of violence
pain and sorrow
they are the ones
who are acting out
the fears and frustrations
of a million
tortured souls
-yeah-
its true
when you look
at your children
you are looking
deep
into your own soul

so whose side ya gonna take?
master or slave

Genuflection for Fun and Profit
or
The Desire to Kow Tow is the Personification of Evil

-'cause you're givin' over your responsibility for yourself to someone else-

-genuflect-
to be servilely obedient or respectful
-kow tow-
to kneel and touch the forehead to the ground in...worship
-overseer-
-supervisor-
an administrative officer in charge of business, government, school unit or
operation

that's where the line is drawn
that's where you and your master meet face to face
-to the demon's minions-

FAIR WARNING

The Psyche of the Individual
or
Ruthless Selfishness Revisited Once Again

while the whole human sensory apparatus
was reflecting the universe
that was god
-original insight-

but as the reflection became more clear and more powerful
it manifest the self
an essential component of language and cultural transmission
the human brain began to reflect
rather than the whole universe
memory
it's own stored images
-itself-
that's self consciousness
-the fall from grace-
creating a symbol for god
which became more important than the real thing
allowing thought to flourish at the expense of vital human tissues
-flesh, blood, and bone-

self consciousness
that was the fall from grace
-the forbidden fruit-

the first division of perception
(between 'me' and the world)
opened pandora's box
and the demons it released are
every self aggrandizing scheme we pursue

by dividing our consciousness
we were able to view ourselves
as a separate entity
central to a world of things and events

when we ordered thought through language
we set in motion
virtually in perpetuity
a machine of constant progression
-the self-

the structure of thought
is ordered by syntax
subject-verb-object

in order to communicate any significant concept
we pretty much have to follow that rule
or a variation thereof

that gets us on the road of cause and effect
which leads to science and technology

the earliest science was probably 'god'
of some form or another
an explanation in search of a question
'cause god can answer 'em all

...or so it would appear...

it is apparent that an intelligence
a universal mind
a wholeness beyond our comprehension
brought forth the universe
Earth and man

universe evolves energy evolves matter evolves
Earth, DNA, man, thought, and our common mind
manifest as our planetary community

note the progression
from static
galaxies, stars, planets
last a long time
to dynamic
fast, furious, ephemeral
human life
the wink of an eye

its that durn progression
-you know-
the one that starts with the big bang
something had to kick it off
and *something* determined it would follow
a certain course, plan, program
the laws of physics and nature
-this is apparent-

equally apparent
is the fact that this 'something'
we can never actually *know*
at least not within those same laws of physics and nature

thought cannot contain a whole perception
if it could then we could reproduce it
write it down and pass it around

which is, basically, what the poets, priests, and politicians
lay claim to
but its ok to try
so long as you don't lie
and there's the rub
the truth is the same for everybody
at least it is for all human beings living on planet Earth

what is truth
is what we may observe with all our senses
-that-
ourselves, our world, and our universe
-is-
a direct, immediate manifestation of that unknowable 'something'

when we store that perception in our brain
as memory
it becomes an aspect of the self
and the symbol becomes more important
than the actuality to which it refers
because thought produces a gross satisfaction
that pure perception may obliterate

immediate, direct perception
may demand an action
that is painful
-a sacrifice-
a sacrifice of the self

its the light of pure perception
that exposes the entire structure of thought
as built on fear
-god, tribe, property-

intelligence knows no god, tribe, or property

clear, clean perception
reveals the essence of thought
as fear

...remember?...
its part of that same progression
-replicator-animal-human-thought-
ya know?
all geared to the same thing
-survival-
to the max
ya know what I'm sayin'?
the fear of death
the primordial motivation of life
the most ancient memory
that guides our existence

kinda like sayin' 'god'
except comin' 'round from the other side
like a dog chasin' it's tail
there is no end to speculatin' 'bout god
its just as enlightening to talk about science fiction
the one extrapolates backward in time
the other extrapolates forward in time

clear, clean, direct, and immediate
-perception-
pure and simple
demands an action that is painful
the sacrifice of the self/god polarity

god ranks second only to me, myself, and I
as the most successful
replication of thought
with property coming in a close third

because god goes beyond death
here and now
-in our imagination-
while the self lives on
-actually-
(the fragmented self of our common mind)
in each of us
and our children
and our children's children

culture- the integrated pattern of human knowledge, belief, and behavior that depends on man's capacity for learning and transmitting knowledge to succeeding generations and/or the customary beliefs, social forms, and material traits of a racial, religious, or social group to paraphrase Webster's:

cultural selection- the cultural process that results in the survival of ideas or belief systems best adjusted to the conditions under which they replicate and that is equally important for the perpetuation of biologically and psychologically gratifying information and the elimination of biologically detrimental and psychologically painful information as it is produced by human experience and variations in neural firing patterns

thought and behavior
-prescribed by culture-
which produces better life
spreads through humanity
and across generations

for primitive man
'better life'
was the same
individually and collectively

successful cultural information
knowledge and technique
rituals, occupations, and pastimes
produced results
essentially equal for everybody

what was good for the individual was good for the tribe
and
what was good for the tribe was good for the individual
for 95% of human history

as the cultural revolutions occur
-agricultural/industrial/technological-
the surplus survival success
-material abundance-
feeds the selfish
who form structures of power
based on techniques and technologies
wielded by authority

the authority and the technology
become more important than people

knowledge and raw materials
take precedence over human life

because fear motivates the most selfish
to wield power
recklessly and ruthlessly
in pursuit of
the ultimate pleasure

fear spreads
and the selfish prosper
at the expense of
intelligence
and the common woman and man
because intelligence is aware
that the price of pleasure is pain

intelligence and fear can't occupy the same space
subvert and subdue intelligence
and fear is free to reign

remember
intelligence guides the universe
but the fear of death
guides man
-its hardwired into our body and brain-
some very few
have accessed intelligence
and lived their lives that way
but the 'self' still rules our common mind

ME, MYSELF, and I

-the most successful replication of thought-

I
Am the Center of the Universe

a genetic survival mechanism of the human brain
a biologically inherited machine of division

The Initiator of Human Behavior
-(don't hide your eyes)-
'because of me'

I am the highest form of the memory that molds matter.

I am the fear of death
made manifest
in the human brain.

To ensure a high probability that I will survive, I have distinguished myself- of all that touches my senses- as being of the highest order. All 'others' are subordinate to 'me'. 'I want what I want when I want it' is my prime directive. How my actions affect the world around me is of no importance unless they directly, immediately benefit me. I want all the best life has to offer- food, sex, and shelter- of only the highest quality.

To this end I ruthlessly seek power in whatever form available that best suits the purpose of my survival to the maximum potential. Intimidation and violence are my first and foremost, swiftest and surest tools for gaining power. To gain power over a stronger opponent, knowledge is the key. My lust for power has used knowledge to create the ability to destroy the whole of human civilization in half an hour through the use of nuclear weapons. None has a greater power than this. For, of the whole of life, I, alone, am most worthy of life, the genetic survival mechanism of the human brain, the most highly evolved creature in the chain of evolution- me.

But wait. There seems to be more than one 'me' runnin' 'round here, over 5 billion more as a matter of fact. All are survival machines. All seek to better ensure their survival by whatever means are necessary as far as their knowledge and opportunity take them. All are me.

Ok, so we don't all have the ability to reach out and initiate armegeddon. Nor are we all mass murderers or rapists or child abusers, corporate executives, preachers, or politicians. But by accepting the present world disorder, we create the conditions in which brutality and tyranny thrive.

When I call myself an american or russian or african, christian, muslim, or buddhist, communist or libertarian, nazi or democrat, I am perpetrating the division and conflict of the world- racial, national, religious, economic, and political- the stuff world wars are fought over- ideas, beliefs, and words. There are those willing to die or sacrifice others to defend their concepts of god, tribe, or property.

When I send my children to public schools to be indoctrinated by the state, I am smothering the spark of intelligence before the flames of awareness, truth, and discontent become an inferno that engulfs the false values of a corrupt society.

When I participate in conversations of rumor, gossip, and prejudice, I am spreading a poison to contaminate all our human relations. When I don't stand up and speak out against prejudice, ignorance, and injustice then I am a participant in a global crime in progress. Future generations will look back at us and say "How could they have let that happen?"- as we do when we look back at slavery and other holocausts.

This is the common mind we all share. It is dominated by a single thought- *me*. All thinking is subordinate to 'I'. Each person's 'I' is only slightly, superficially different, colored by particular memories, cultures, climate, food geography, family, but essentially, each is of the same origin- the fear of death.

Thought has created a static, permanent entity in a universe where nothing perceived by the senses is actually static or permanent.

another interlude

the life of woman and man
revolves less than a hundred times
'round the sun

human thought
in the wink of an eye

-perception-
the speed of light

and gone again as if they had never been

—-

-our whole planetary community-
not only we are connected psychologically via our common mind
-the human brain-
we are now connected physically via technology
not only may I see and hear instantly anywhere on the planet
I may also be seen and heard
not only may I instantly access all information available anytime anywhere
I may also actually physically appear at any site on the globe within a day

its like intelligence
-the spirit of god-
the universal mind
is reachin' 'round
from behind us
tappin' us on the shoulder
and sayin'
"Hey Bud, check it out, I'm right here, lookin' through your eyes."

when we become
wholly conscious
then we'll be
wholly conscious
of each other
-everybody at once-
this is it
here and now

reiteratin'

through perception, logic, and memory
knowledge and technique accumulated
providing a vast amount of survival success
and psychological satisfaction

all of what was feared
the unknown
and ultimately uncontrollable
-death-
was deferred to god
of some form or another

so what we know
are the things
thought thinks about
and what we don't know
is god

the more we know
the more thought thinks about
the more we divide the world
'till we can damn near pick it apart and put it back together
but today we are collectively more savage than any animal that ever
existed
with super computers
to do our thinking
and
high tech weapons
that kill multitudes from great distances
and
machines that run, swim, and fly
to a degree no biological entity will ever hope to achieve
and
a capacity and seeming predilection
for genocides and mass infanticides and world wide wars

today thought is more powerful
than it ever has been before
and the world
is in a more precarious position
than it ever has been before

intelligence:
the ability to learn or understand
or to deal with new or trying situations

thought is not intelligent in itself
thought is an extension
of the animal instinct
a biological psychic reaction

simple observation is intelligence
perception
is lined up directly
with the universal mind
-the spirit of god-

intelligence may utilize thought out of necessity
'cause thought is the most powerful tool we possess

but thought
left unattended by observation
feeds on itself
through human lives and events
and grows into a whirlwind of destruction

"JUST CALL ME...

thought is the ultimate tool
for manipulating the world
producing
physical and psychological gratification

the tool that bore all tools
creates an effect
a chain reaction
of human thought and behavior
immediately and through generations
and establishes itself as authority
a force violent
in cause and effect
which rules the world

the vehicle of thought's influence is *culture*
psychological archetypes
replicating and variegating
through our common mind
and human behavior
across the planet and over time

...LUCIFER."

BOOK FIVE

not a new world order
but a whole new world

an end to the cause and effect semi-consciousness
that orders our society
and the emergence of a consciousness
of the wholeness of life

ONE WORLD

is enough
for all
of us

This is an unprecedented moment of human evolution.

the human being is out on the frontier
of the evolution of life

the transformation occurring now
is as significant a step
in the course of evolution
as was the step
from primordial worm
to modern man

this is a step in the sequence of
inanimate matter-animate matter-consciousness

from simple one celled organisms
to the systems of organs that create a human being
to the system of conscious humans that create a whole planetary
community

we are only a half a moment away
from full consciousness
or death
whichever comes first

its coming about the same way
the universe and life have always evolved
as if the universe passionately desired
to achieve full consciousness

explosion:
a large-scale, rapid, and spectacular expansion, outbreak, or upheaval
synergy:
combined action or operation
synergism:
interactions of discrete agencies (as industrial firms) or agents (as drugs)
such that the total effect is greater than the sum of the individual effects

An explosive synergism characterizes the present unprecedented planetary
crisis.

the intelligence which informed the energy that guided matter through
space and time
to planet Earth is the same intelligence which brought us forth is the same
intelligence
which is drawing out a full blown consciousness from the human brain

The Principle of Polarity in the Evolution of Consciousness

-culture divides while technology unifies-

the self
as concepts of god and property
transmitted through cultural selection
divides the world

The variety of clothing, hairstyle, persona, performance, food preparation, ritual, pastime, occupation, art, dance, music, knowledge, and spiritual expression- the whole of human culture- is the very core and source of beauty and the best of human relationship. There is no awareness of beauty without contrast. Each cultural expression plays it's own part. Each part has it's own intrinsic value. Every facet of human expression fits the environment in which it originated like a key fits a lock- planet Earth and the whole of humanity. But at this point of human evolution, to identify oneself completely with any particular culture or environmental influence is to separate oneself from all others. To judge any fragment as being inherently better or worse it to create conflict.

Its as the technology created expanded population
the world over
and achieved instantaneous global communications
and cultural programming
has covered the surface of the Earth
intruding it's influence into every corner of the globe
that each culture comes into contact
with all the others
and the fragmented self of our common mind
in every nation, of every religion, and all races
finds it's boundaries closing in
becoming more definite, constraining, and in constant conflict
with the different aspects of itself
creating chaos in human relationship
and the shocking abuse of the environment
and the interrelatedness of all things
events, ideas, and people
becomes apparent
and central
to the perception
of the human brain.

-OUR COMMON MIND-

The Interrelatedness of All Things, People, Events, and Ideas

-a consciousness of the wholeness of life-

except for the apparent and utterly mysterious major discontinuities
in the evolution of the universe and life
(the big bang-replication)
all that we observe can be traced through a cause and effect sequence
(at least to hear us tell it)
backward and forward in time

but what we are experiencing now has reached a level of complexity
that is essentially overwhelming the senses
as we approach another major discontinuity- full consciousness
there are so many causes and effects acting on each other
from every angle intertwined with so many other causes and effects
that we finally realize tracing them to their origins
and determining there relationships
is meaningless

when you're done you aint got nothin' but a memory

-that's why intelligence demands simple observation-

Chaos In All It's Glory

Dividing all the parts of the world and naming them and symbolizing processes and reactions and determining their relationships has gone about as far as its gonna go within the constraints of self, god, and property. That type of semi-consciousness has created this world that's collapsing in on itself. Its just like Einstein said we can't solve our problems at the same level of consciousness that created them.

As we have evolved we have altered our world. At first slowly, we produce small changes. Technique, beneficial and life enhancing, evolving from the observation of nature- agriculture- radically alters human society and initiates growth and alters the environment. New knowledge produces the technology of metal, again spurring growth and the exploitation of resources natural and human, affecting further our physical environment and our human relationships causing a need for new techniques technologies which begin to radically influence all areas of life at an ever increasing scope of dimension and accelerating pace of change.

Technology affects population affects technology causes assault on natural resources requires new technologies which in turn affects population and pollution and resources and every aspect of human relationship is under siege.

All these changes create waves of influence, the waves overlap, interference waves are created, events change more, unexpected consequences result, initiating further waves that alter the original events which produce new reactions that create new pressures that call forth new responses which have unforeseen effects on the initial causes.

This is the reflection of the functioning of the human brain, the manifestation of human behavior initiated by thought... a deteriorating process of thought revealed by our electronic nervous system, that is the most blatant manifestation of our common mind.

the only thought
that has *any*
absolute value
the only thought that is good
the only thought that is necessary
is
rational, logical, scientific
-*that* thought is aligned with intelligence-
the whole of technique

the thought that is not good
is the thought that is rooted in fear
-in concepts of god and property-

seeking pleasure and avoiding pain
-our primitive self-
the self corrupts the use of our tools
-our technology-
and completely contaminates our environment
-natural, physical, social, psychological-
local and global

our rational thought has recently been short circuited through technology
-television-
mass global communications
controlled by the self of our common mind

so many simultaneous connections
are being made
without the proper preparations
and distributions of material and energy
that it appears the worlds fixin' ta catch a fire

with gutenberg's invention the print media exercised the mind
and sharpened and clarified thought to the point of today's high tech
world

print media forced humans to sit still and quiet for long periods of time
the reader is disciplined
to discern and make discrete distinctions
simultaneously on different levels
from the actual form of print on paper
to remaining objective
to separate fact and logic from style and tone
to intuit the speakers attitude
and to test the truth or false
against one's own perception

and television has eliminated *all* that

Conversation in a Room Full of Mirrors

in today's world
the purpose of the media
is to force a lie
aka advertising (bald faced lies)
and your local and world news (omission of significant facts and context
lies)

unpleasant fact, thought, and emotion
is counteracted with image and sound
the symbolic outweighs the actual
-imagination replaces reality-

the revolution has not been televised
but every thought we think is

Psychologists estimate a person thinks some 50,000 thoughts a day, the same ones over and over, day after day, with only the slightest of variations. The thoughts our common mind thinks are being pumped back at us relentlessly through the screens big and small- sitcoms, soaps, drama, adventure, horror, comedy, porn, nature, science, sports, music videos, hollywood movies, and infinite advertising.

the thought
that our common mind thinks
determines our behavior
both individual and collective
and our behavior determines
the quality of our life and world

there has been so much programming for so many years
we have been scraping the bottom of the barrel
-a barrel that is our brain turned inside out-
our common mind

the television has created for us
processes of thought
-paradigms and presuppositions-
that produce mass mental incoherence
and behavior
that is powerless
to effect positive change

information overload

the video screen provides
a non-stop parade of pictures
and silly slogans
that bear no relevance
to our daily life
-information we haven't asked for-
a series of flashing images bearing no relationship to each other
or anything else
but triggers in us the emotion we crave
in our passive existence
requiring no rational thought
-matter of fact-
the television requires we not be concerned or compassionate
that we make no connections or understand implications
that we have no sense of history
television requires that the images that hypnotize
bear no relationship to our actual personal lives

and the sad fact is we accept this as a matter of course
indeed
we don't even see the danger of the trivial pursuit of the video screen
that dominates our culture

the original mass communicators
had limited reach and a small audience
cave paintings, sculpture, music, dance
creation myths and the human drama
evolved into
the display of the persona,
the impetus of Gutenberg,
and the demand for image consultants

the initiators of glorious innocence
-the whole of art-
the spirit of god acting through man
putting everything in order and in it's proper place
-so intoxicated by the truth of existence-
have evolved into today's mass communicators
to whom only image is all
insight ignored
emotion glorified
and actual utility has become secondary
appearance more valuable than substance
and the corpses that implies

It is no longer a matter of the perception of truth being communicated from sender too receiver- individual to individual, individual to group, and back again- it is now a matter of emotion, pleasure, and pain being communicated. At the dawn of civilization the receiver slowly, tentatively, absorbed the information that improved life- culture- and each generation of artists and craftsmen and observers of the world made improvements and passed them on- until today- we have created a synergistically strange feedback loop where there is an almost immediate and constant interaction between sender and receiver- sender influences receiver and the very same time the receiver is reaching out to influence the sender in ever tighter loops producing a self contained resonance that threatens to shatter the natural and social environment.

Human behavior has become increasingly absurd- an absurdity that borders on the pathological. The process has been so insidious and incestuous that the radically deviant personalities, right along with the so-called morally acceptable and socially respectable preachers, politicians, ceo's, managers, and other white collar criminals feel compelled to commit scandals and crimes both petty and atrocious, public and private, to insinuate themselves into our consciousness, either directly or indirectly. They feel its the only way to transform their petty existence- nothing is real 'til its been televised- the same means and motivation as the terrorist.

We cause them to act out, through our own sick need to be entertained. We seek a violent stimulus to arouse our jaded senses.

The alienated personality- an alienation born of woman's and man's separation from the land and their separation from the product of their craft with the division of labor of the industrial revolution and the separation from their neighbors and their community in the urban jungle and now the separation from their thought and perception being done by computers and television- *pervades our society.*

The self of our common mind, fragmented, seeks integration.

the breakdown of the boundaries
-the barriers that separate us-
are the birth pains
of a revolution in progress

the interrelatedness of all things
is in our face
forcing us to confront the facts
and participate in a large scale integration

———

we have spent the evolution of a species
first observing a whole world
then breaking it down
smaller and smaller
naming each part
tracing it's origin
and noting it's cause and effect relationships
as best we can

and you see what we have created

the process has allowed us previously unimagined feats of power
-the process of thought-

but it has been at a cost we have yet to face
-death-

we have faced outwardly for so long that we have forgotten
-the face of god-

and she demands to be seen

images, memory, neural firing patterns in the human brain order our
perceptions
inward symbols exclude outward actuality
creating deep division and blindness
-demanding only one action-
see the whole world
-undivided-
that's what love is

and that's freedom from slavery
and rather than being a slave to the power that rules the Earth
-the self-
the whole process of thought
-our common mind-
that power becomes slave to us serving quickly and efficiently our every
need

BOOK SIX

the indivisible whole

the creation of the one world
occurring now
-large scale integration-
is fixin' ta produce
a major shock wave
through our home and family
body and mind
-the one we all share-
as the self lays down to die
-that's me-

the me sitting here now
the me that's hardwired into every human brain
the me that is violence
-the me that fears death-
the violence that is the dominating factor in human relationship
where money is the medium
and television the principle tool

it goes somethin' like this here
the world is a being that consists of competing systems of power
structures
that are composed of organizations of groups and individuals

the world is not at ease with itself
a being that is diseased
and divided

and like all life forms
the world has a built in defense mechanism
-an immune system-
that kicks in naturally
to direct the energy and resources of the organism to promote health

the whole world acting as one
-a large scale integration-
that's what the present circumstances demand

the creation of a new being
another dimension of energy/matter in space/time
the next continuum of consciousness

the one world immune system
the mechanism for health
-large scale integration-
that's like where the big fish eat the little fish
right on up to the top of the food chain
where the biggest depends on the smallest
ya know, like
the whale eats plankton

the systems that determine our lives
the power structures we depend on for survival
national, religious, economic, industrial, etc.
in their turn depend on the mass of little people for their survival
if the regular folks are diminished or hurt or weak or diseased
then it affects the largest power structures
-just wait and see-

that's why the laborer demands an immediate reckoning
and that reckoning occurs simply as seeing 'what is'
all boundaries and division
-inward and outward-
between and within people
are man made
created and preserved
by the self
-our common mind fragmented-

large scale integration removes barriers, ends conflict and competition
by revealing through technological and organizational processes
that we are all working together
the same way for the same goals
its the scientific, technological thought
-the whole of technique-
that is our common ground
regardless of politics, ideology, religion, or national division
the same technological procedures
apply to our human needs the world over

the successful systems in today's world
are setting aside the market mechanism
and using technique to control
not only material resources and their uses
but also to control prices and individual economic behavior
the problem with this is that its strictly in the service of big money
-that's where the power is-
and relegates the role of the individual
to what is, essentially, slavery

big business is involved with government
government is involved with lawyers
lawyers are involved with big business
big money is involved with it all

laborers depend on big business
big business depends on wall street
-capital-
and madison avenue
-media-
(the manipulation of the masses)
and consumers who are 90% laborers

big money depends on
mass consuming tax payers
and cheap labor

government mandates education
education mandates social structure
social structure mandates human value
and so-called morality
and the most respectable
and socially acceptable
is big money

lawyers unify big business
big business breaks unions
forms new alliances
and temporary employment agencies

government mandates education
big business intrudes on education
big business and government intrude on third world nations
through greed for cheap labor and natural resources
and big money is the means and motivation

and the laborers are losin' out

the laborers are taxed by government
and charged by big business
and molded by education
and exploited by lawyers
and looked down upon by social services
and pressured by health care

the boundaries of big business have expanded exponentially
encompassing nations at every level of government
reaching in and manipulating the core of our existence
through every avenue of human relationship
with police, politicians, preachers, educators, and marketing experts
all in the mix
and the technology of television

Corporate and government forces nurture profit at the expense of human life- as if it were right and education takes place without consulting the parent. That's how children are taught- to accept as normal exploitation, ignorance, and brutality- so that when they begin to struggle with their own self reliance they will accept without question their own slavery to the force of evil that rules the world. The primary tool used to keep the people down is debt bondage.

The pay we receive as laborers steadily diminishes in proportion to the price we have to pay to live and support our families with housing, food, clothes, utilities, insurance, and transportation. Our employment opportunities have become steadily fewer. The job market is described as it has been recently designed- temporary- to satisfy big business' greed for cheap labor. The temporary employment service represents the most atrocious crime of all- slavery.

The growth of the temporary employment agencies and the experience of working for them is a book in itself. You can't imagine it. Number one, if you need immediate employment you have few choices- one of the forty temp services in town gonna put you to work. That is the one and only positive benefit for the laborer. Going out on the job and depending on the temp service for your livelihood is another matter. You do the same job as the permanent employees and receive dollars less per hour and no benefits. You are not guaranteed a permanent job. Temporary assignments can last years or you may spend years trying to luck on to a job compatible with your abilities. And ya gotta accept what they give ya 'cause its the only game in town. Unless you got the time and resources to submit applications and resumes and sit and wait for someone to call, someone who probably already got plenty temps already workin' and you better have a helluva experience and references to beat 'em out. I have seen that take years too. But, whatever, your needs and concerns are not factors in the equation that results in employment. Ya just gotta scuffle for the scraps.

until the head
-big money-
feels the pain
of it's body
-laborers-
and accounts in it's plan of expansion
for the integration of the individual
its gonna get awful hard to breathe
and the blood circulating to the brain
is gonna get cut off
and
our one world
-the whole body/mind/environment-
will fail

rational thought arises naturally, spontaneously out of observation
the clearer the perception, the more scientific the thought that arises

our mass communication is a manifestation of our common consciousness
our mass communication, media of every form, is a reflection of ourselves
the images the media presents are a mass of contradiction
-hollywood fantasy, advertising, prominent personalities, news of the
world
especially the third world characterized by starvation and war-
and what is of significance is trivialized and what is trivial is glorified

GAWK
-to stare stupidly-
it aint perception - it aint observation

the media is a reflection of ourselves
we have cultivated a gawker mentality
all we wanna focus on is sex, violence, and scandal
the absurd human behavior and the gawker mentality feed on each other
-the more we gawk the more we have to gawk at-
we appear to create media events
-war, crime, and violence-
to trigger our emotion
but when it comes to lookin' at ourselves
and lookin' at ourselves in the world
we're like the ostrich stickin' it's head in the sand
and while our head is buried
our ass shinin' in the sun
and the lion creepin' up from behind
maybe that's givin' god something to gawk at

and that's kinda sad
that one of the major aspects of culture that we share globally
is the media / gawker polarity
-but there is a seed of beauty there-
its that we may use our electronic nervous system to saturate our common
mind
with a message of love

BOOK SEVEN

Global Sorrow, Authority, and the Mind of the Child

though we may see outwardly
-if we bother to look at the whole picture and ourselves in it-
the greatest changes in human history goin' on all around us
we seem to act as if we are not part of it
as if it were all happening beyond our control

but buddy I'm here to tell ya
look right down there
at that nose on yo face
-its as obvious as that-

did ya ever notice there's a connection there
between ya hand and ya head?
yeah?
well
it just so happens
there is a connection
between yourself and the world

you're connected to the whole world, not just your usual, familiar corner
of it

I wonder why we do not ceaselessly question our existence
when we look at the stars in the sky,
when our children exhibit their pain and confusion,
when we witness the atrocities of poverty and war on a global scale
or
when the first shades of green,
on a warm, sunny, spring day,
light up the grass and shrubs
beneath the barren trees
through which the light blue sky and billowing clouds hug the earth
and the cool breeze carries the sweet, pungent scent of fresh growth
and the earth throbs with a new found energy
or
when the destruction of the environment
threatens the whole of life on the planet

Is there, simply, no wonder or concern at all? Or is our wonder and concern buried by our selfish pursuits, or vaporized by fear and ignorance? Or have tradition and belief poisoned the seed of inquiry before it could grow? Or are we unaware that our life and health is dependent upon the well being of the whole world? Are we actually unaware of the facts and their implications? Awareness of the facts is a burning passion, an endless drive to revolution.

The United Nations has reported hundreds of millions of children, worldwide, labor as virtual slaves, in untold pain- deformity, disease, death, and unimaginable loneliness- will you allow yourself to be fully conscious of that?

Manifestations of individual suffering are obvious, everyday events in our world- death and dismemberment in battles of civil, tribal, regional political, and religious wars, terrorism, political oppression, starvation, poverty, homelessness, joblessness, accidents in the home and on the job and on the road, alcoholism, drug addiction, criminal activities, dysfunctional families, mental and physical disease, injustice and inequality, uncontrollable emotion and unrequited love- the list goes on and on of different forms of sorrow which touch every person's life. To the naming of problems there is no end. And this is the world we have created for our children.

The development of our mind occurs not only as evolution, but perhaps more profoundly during the course of childhood. An individual is born with only 25% of the brains ultimate growth. The most significant period of development is in the first two years after birth.

What should we teach the children? God? Country? Race? If so, what is it we will say about these matters? We must tell the children the whole truth.

LOOK INTO YOUR OWN SOUL

The pollution of our mind begins in childhood by the parents, (no offense mom) with the fears, traditions, anxieties, beliefs, prejudices, and idiosyncrasies that were taught them in their turn by their parents. Granted, for the majority of people, there has been no evil intent- but the result remains the same.

Children are perfect learning machines- in spite of what some ignorant parents, teachers, and assorted adults would have you believe- children have clean, unconditioned minds- the most magnificent creation of the universe.

A human beings brain succumbs to a degree of conditioning from the moment the senses come into contact with the world. The most powerful conditioning factor is the child's primary care givers- mainly the parents and siblings, then the rest of the family, the baby sitter and the TV. Whatever the parents are- that will be the children. The children reflect perfectly the environment, dominated by the parents and the culture in which they are raised. So when it seems like there may be something wrong with the kids- there most likely is. Just remember who created and raised them.

There is something primal about power over others, but you might not have noticed unless you had power wielded over yourself, like all children have, and if the power is destructive- and most is- *because it forces human beings to fit into this mess-* then that will be the power that the child will plug into and get off on over others.

the white man determines the system by which we are judged
-socially, morally, financially, and judicially-
he creates and operates the machine of society
-schools, factories, courts, prisons, armies-
he forces our children
at a certain time, on a certain date, at a certain place
to begin a process of education
-an education by which he sets the standard and brands each child with his grade-

were he not able to do this
-with our cooperation-
he would not be able to control world affairs
for his benefit, at our expense

the child is taken out of her home, away from her family
into an environment controlled by big strangers
who instruct behavior and thought
all day long for at least a dozen years

the instruction of behavior and thought
ingrains in the child's brain
the structure of authority

the child learns her program from the powers that be
-big business-
television, advertising, sports, hollywood movies
-government-
from schools to the police to the president
-religious organizations-
from catholic to muslim

the authorities grade and classify each child
and ranks them in the structure
created by authority

school teaches nothing of truth, intelligence,
or how to live righteously
or how to determine
high quality, good morality, and absolute value
-or what is actually happening in the world or our relationship to that-
more than that, school obscures these aspects of life
because confronting them would be to demand their action of
responsibility

in school
were you ever told the plight of third world nations,
the true causes,
or our relationship to those countries?
did they ever explain any of our actions there other than
foreign aid for economic and technological development?
did your teachers ever explain
covert operations to overthrow governments,
or military aid to dictators to squash revolts,
or which corporations operated in the third world,
the reasons why they were there,
exactly what their activities were,
and the implications and consequences of those activities?

I didn't think so

did anyone ever explain the pledge of allegiance
what it means or why we say it
at an age we could hardly understand what's goin' on anyway?

did anyone ever let you know
that the declaration of independence demands
we abolish any government that is destructive
to life, liberty, and the pursuit of happiness?

human society puts a heavy mark on the child's mind
when we become aware of the quality of this mark
we will erase it and not allow another

with no marks on their mind
like prison bars in their eyes
the child will come to understand
the infinite possibilities of each moment
and that only one will be reality

and they will know
that what they see with their mind
and what they create with their hand
will be their whole life

and that we share this reality
with the Whole Earth

and that the closest connection we have
with the spirit of god
-intelligence-
is found in the mirror of human relationship

technology of the highest is here now
thus it is not knowledge we seek
but healthy human contact
-love-

the essence of what we're talkin' 'bout
is we live in a divided, deteriorating world
and we are the cause of it

the kids of today are letting us know
they understand what society values
-where do you think so many of them get the idea life has no value?-

the stress of living in poverty
is like a cancer
that consumes people
right on through generations

human beings face
an evolutionary challenge
of the same nature
as the one the dinosaurs faced
before their extinction

how to adapt to rapid radical changes in the whole living environment

the power structures that control our lives
and our whole world
are violent

why do we act surprised
when the violence reaches street level?

the suppressed rage emerges
in human relationship
in public and private
collectively and individually
casually, intensely, ritualistically, and intimately

in america
street gangs are the most graphic example
of the expression of humanities deepest psyche
they have fully assimilated the culture in which they were born
they're just like miniature worlds between themselves
power structures in competition
over territory and resources

The Need for Human Contact
-Strong as Hunger-

on up to the psychological hunger
the slavery to image
that rules human relationship
brought about by the media/entertainment industry
-that's how we learn to judge each other-

if you can't afford expensive things
then you're treated bad by society
if you can afford them, then you risk robbery

and if ya aint got no bad attitude ya might get dissed to the max

what's so killin' 'bout it is
our willingness to enslave ourselves
-or rather, our keen desire to do so-

the dominant planetary culture
-america-
sets the stage for our alienated youth

its that part of being human that cries out for dignity and respect
that produces the current hardcore street attitude
-out of conditions that have been intended to wipe out that part of our
humanity-
which just makes it come out that much harder and stronger
-self defense is not violence-

if you feel the need
to holler and scream and curse your children on a regular basis
or at the other extreme
let them run wild in the street
then you've gone too far
and ya better look at the whole thing that's happenin'
-where it comes from and where its goin'-

before it comes back 'round at ya

BOOK EIGHT

The Color of God and the Substance Thereof

or

The Revolutionary Act of Doing Nothing

or

Polarity and Paradox

-containing the contradiction without conflict-

Whenever a number of like items are grouped together, a small percent of them will account for almost all of the groups significance.

Vilfredo Pareto

Men first feel necessity, then look for utility, next attend to comfort, still later amuse themselves with pleasure, then grow dissolute in luxury, and finally go mad and waste their substance.

Giambattista Vico

Politicians...may reiterate a thousand times that the basis of the new world order must be universal respect for human rights, but it will mean nothing as long as this imperative does not derive from the respect of the miracle of being, the miracle of the universe, the miracle of nature, the miracle of our own existence. Only someone who submits to the authority of the universal order can genuinely value himself and his neighbors, and thus honor their rights as well.

Vaclav Havel

or
as that old Indian philosopher once said
"The no-mind no-thinks no-thoughts about no-things."

-the true individual is our common mind undivided-

on the substance of intelligence
and
the matter of belief
and
the fact of death

our responsibility

When I send my children to school, essentially handing them over to strangers who have free reign to mold their minds, I am unequivocally involved in our system of indoctrination into the power's structure. When I go to the grocery store and buy over processed and chemically laden food to eat and feed my family I am irrevocably involved with the petrochemical industry and the corporate run farms. When I pay my taxes to fund covert wars overseas, I share responsibility for decimating members of my human family. When i vote in an election I am supporting the corruption perpetrated by our public officials, the pawns of the military-industrial complex. When I pay my utility bills and buy gas for my car I am raping and poisoning the earth hand in hand with the energy corporations.

The whole business is like the persecution of the Jews under Hitler and we say "How could the German citizens let that happen?" And I say how is it that we can create this god forsaken world every day? We create with our thought and behavior.

The individual is not separate from society, nor does society exist other than as the collective individual. We are fearful, confused human beings living in a diseased, deteriorating world. The disease and the division originate in the replication of thought in human brain cells. The most successful replications of thought are the self, god, property, and the whole of technique.

the matter of belief

The self is the most common and the most powerful divider of the person and the world. Next in power and position is god. God goes deeper in the mind than property. Rich and poor alike will worship the same god, and go to war allied against other believers of other gods. Much more rarely do the poor band together against the rich, even while the rich are already banded together against the poor.

It is the conditioning of our minds to accept the god of whatever culture we may have found ourselves in that sets the stage for the imposition of authority. A conditioning so thorough that we find it hard to accept others of not the same belief. Once we have allowed our mind to accept as true, something that is absolutely undetectable, not subject to proof, and utterly superstitious- then we have opened the door for authority to step in and implant the thoughts that it sees as fit for it's own survival. The thought that authority sees fit to enforce is the concept of property.

belief is a process of thought
-a particular neural firing pattern in the brain-
thus it is subject to matter

and all matter
is born of the stellar dust
created by the big bang

and of what does this stardust
-out of which was created the human being-
consist?

...nothing...

Modern science tells us the universe is created out of nothing. There is no particular substance to the essence of matter.

You may have heard of something called an atom, which consists of a nucleus of protons and neutrons orbited by electrons. The atom was supposed to be the building block out of which was made all that we perceive.

First consider the size of an atom. Imagine the head of a pin. Now imagine the head of pin- hollow- the size of planet earth- filled with golf balls. The number of golf balls that it would take to fill the earth is the number of atoms in the head of a pin.

Now consider the main ingredient of an atom- empty space. Imagine a hollow steel ball the size of a hot air balloon. If it were a single atom, the nucleus in the center would be the size of a grain of sand, vibrating at velocities that approach the speed of light, while the shell would be created by orbiting electrons the size of fine dust particles.

thus
looking outwardly
through space to the stars
and inwardly to the atom
we see the universe
consists of 99% empty space
and all that we see is alive
permeated with an intense energy

but scientists probing the inside of atoms now say
that even the protons, neutrons, and electrons
are not *things* but *events*
which show only tendencies to exist
or
are actually relationships between patterns of energy
that space and time and all that they encompass are not separate
but form an unbroken wholeness

we
who are only extremely complicated
highly ordered combinations
of the same stardust
are nothing

116

close your eyes
come on now
just close your eyes
for 3 full seconds

that's it

ok
now
that moment
when you focused
momentarily
on the visual aspect
of closed eyes

shifting patterns of light and color
against a deep, vibrant background
of velvet black

go ahead
take another look

that's the void in which the universe appears
that's right
the very same one that is the night sky

that's the universe
inward and outward
yeah
you know
when you close your eyes
or you're really tryin' to figure somethin' out
that's on the inside

the outside
...well...
that's everything that touches your senses
everything you see, and all you hear, and everything you touch, taste, and
smell
that's the whole perception
...hmmm...
now where does all that come together?
ok
now I remember
-on the inside-
in the brain
the focal point of the whole sensory apparatus

the universe
an infinitely vast void
-darkness-
the ground of being

with exploding flashes
of spacetime energy fluctuations
we call matter

the void
dark and infinite
what we came out of
and
where we're goin' to

that's our
consciousness
in
common

and she is black

its all that jumpin' around and talkin' shit and clashin' tryin' to outshine
for all the attention
and gettin' really radical
building immensely powerful contraptions exceedingly dangerous
and fightin'
and stealin'
and an infinite immaturity

that's like the male/positive principle
as opposed to the female/negative principle

its the male that's forever growin' hard and strong
and pushin' ever forward
steady tryin' ta start somethin'
-*technology*-

and wouldn't *none* of that be happenin'
if the female had not already been there
-mature-
watching and waiting
-*perception*-

THOUGHT
THE GOD

that's what man's been tryin' to do. figure it all out while eating up every
part of the world possible. and the *self* grows. that's what makes the
world small. figurin' it all out- the technique- makes the world small by
makin' survival supremely successful thus the population explosion plus
technology makes possible instant access to everything on the planet and
the potential to create anything. and as is it's nature- to survive to the
max- the self has gone wild- consuming the environment in a process of
destruction, poison, and waste. same way on the inside. close your eyes
again except this time close them for 15 seconds. if you will pay attention
you will notice that all of a sudden, without your volition or your full
awareness that vast space was suddenly filled with thought- a waste of our
substance...

CONSCIOUSNESS
THE GODDESS

don't have to worry 'bout what man's gonna do anyway. she's the eternal
black, he's just a flash. man may eat up the world but he'll never finish
eatin' the goddess- the substance of the universe- because she's no thing-
she's the void of our common consciousness. she's not thought she's
perception. she's the death of the self. the self is born of the fear of
death, remember? the primordial memory- replication

its that polarity again
ya know
where one has no meaning except in relation to the other

if the male/positive principle
-the spur to creation-
matter replicating
is the spark of life
then the eternal origin of the universe
-the source of all-
is out of death
-after all, where were you before you were born?-
that's the female/negative principle
the vast black
silent space
that contains
and allows
the infinite potential
of all that is possible
-that's our common consciousness-

that's our consciousness in common
yeah
that's right
the same one you glimpsed
when you first closed your eyes
and
the same one that is the night sky

the ground of being
-the source of all-
consciousness
the universal substance
sub- means underneath
stance- means to stand
-to stand underneath-
to *understand* is
-the substance of the universe-
consciousness
a silent perception

-that's death-
the self
having served it's purpose of survival
gives way
to nature
-the universal order-

120

death
hey!
what can I say?
its what the essence of the universe finally comes down to
its where everybody meets
that's ok
its not part of the illusion
its where everything becomes real
what it is
in truth
no thing

its what makes life
whole and vital

knowing not death we know not life

and that's 'cause its a subject we mention even more rarely than
the condition of the world and our relationship to it
or our responsibility

probably 'cause they're all related
yeah
I'd say so
I'd say that the self
-the spearhead of thought-
absolutely refuses death
and that's the essence of ignorance
-to ignore-
but then, thought is not perception, anyway

our life cannot be whole
without an immediate, intense, and intimate
awareness of death

death automatically puts our life in perspective
-where pure perception is, the self is not-
without pure perception
the self is all and everything
operating our body, mind, and life
and runnin' the world man has created
-this living hell-

death is the background
against which the self may be observed
-in it's proper perspective-

just close your eyes
and
take a look
yep
that's right
death/responsibility/the world
those three are closely related

at one end of the spectrum
death
the negative polarity
our common consciousness
the ground from which thought arises
-yeah, right there behind your eyes-
the womb out of which life is born
the vast black in which stars explode
the spacetime continuum
out of which matter and energy emerge

mater, mother, matter, material
whatever
its all the same
the whole world
life
the other end of the spectrum
the positive polarity
-insight-
the power or act of seeing into a situation
-penetration-

and in between
life and death
is the world
-our responsibility-
the self

responsible means:
liable to be called on to answer
or
liable to be called to account as the primary cause, motive, or agent

the world emerges out of the universe, replicators grow out of the planet
perception arises with consciousness, and thought is generated by the
brain
perception ends thought- the flame of insight burns away the self
leaving only the scientific method- technology

122

and that's the demand- the responsibility of the individual
to clear out and clean her or his consciousness
through simple observation- immediately
to burn away what is false

the significance of the individual is planetary
because
our world is a creation of our mind
the inward and the outward
they're both the same

we have yet to observe
immediately, intensely, and intimately
the workings of our own mind
-we lack insight-
ergo
the inward we ignore
forces itself outwardly
into our consciousness
through fear and violence
and the division of the world
by the self, god, and property

the action of the individual is
planetary
'cause gettin' yourself together
-and your house, and your neighborhood, and your whole community-
and cleanin' up the whole world
its all the same
your life
is
your part of the world

<u>THE INDIVIDUAL'S DIRECT PERCEPTION</u>
<u>IS THE POWER</u>
<u>INTELLIGENCE COMMANDS</u>

one more time
programs, presupposition, paradigm, prejudice
that's what our self is
fifty thousand thoughts a day
the same ones over and over
producing our action in the world
and where those thoughts come from
and where they're goin'
-the ground out of which they arise-
we ignore
death
should we view our self from the ground
our ignorance is revealed
immediately eliminated
by the simplest of actions
-observation-
that which is unobserved inwardly
forces itself into our consciousness outwardly
and that's the world we live in
and then we say "wow! its terrible! we should do this about that!" and on
and on
in circles gettin' nowhere but deeper in the shit. or we say
"that's life, nothin' I can do about it"
there's nothing I can do about it
because I am the cause
of this whole mess

"I"
am the fear of death
I can do nothing
no thing

PERCEPTION IS THE ACTION

that's the universal mind probing our common spacetime continuum
if ya look all around ya 'fore ya step inta the street
-ya already know what ta do-
if the traffic zippin' by a hundred miles an hour
-ya stop right there-
thinkin' has nothin' ta do with right action
thinkin' has somethin' ta do with communicatin'
-measurement, analysis, testing, symbolizing, extrapolating-
and technique
but right and wrong
and life and death
are no-brainers
if ya stop ta think 'bout 'em
ya probably done missed the mark

OUR COMMON MIND REVISITED AND REITERATED

The Responsibility of the Individual
and
The Revolutionary Act of Doing Nothing

-the more nothing you do the greater it's effect in the world-

and so it came to pass
for the human organism
that the head should control the body
a few folks at the top, land owners, governments, and big business control
the masses
the laborers, the soldiers, agriculture, service, and industry
by means of thought
concepts of property, ownership established by military might- ideas of
tribe, clan, and nation
beliefs of god, duty, honor- emotional triggers of fear, greed, and envy

I tell you
we share a common mind
just as surely as our hands connect to our arms
my mind is connected to yours
and yours to everybody else
and theirs to mine

we share a common mind
outwardly
as our high tech electronic communications system
-and the rest of the mass media-
and inwardly we are connected
via a dimension
which transcends
this spacetime continuum
-death-

we share a common mind
just as surely as
the brains encased within our skulls
are of the same nature,
perform the same function,
and share the same origin

The Revolutionary Act of Doing Nothing

and while you're doing nothing
take a moment
to look around at the world
and your own life
simple observation
without judgment, sentiment, fear, or internal machinations of
manipulation
-without desire-
observation of fact
seeing simply the way things be
-understanding what is-
perception

when I observe the world
and the cosmos which contains it
-with the most technologically advanced scientific equipment that exists-
I see
that the main ingredient of the universe
-from inside the hardest diamond and across a million galaxies-
is 99% empty space
-nothing-

that's the universe
flashing lights and eternal flames in the vast black

the individual-the common man-the laborer
carries the weight of the whole world

AUTHORITY DEMANDS IT MUST BE SO

and that's what makes the action
(or non-action, as the case may be)
of the individual
planetary
its the mass of humanity who labor
always runnin'
and under the gun
-the flesh-
that supports, operates, and maintains
the corrupt authority

that's the power intelligence commands
the mass of humanity
-through the individual's direct perception-
in line with the momentum of the universe
the next step of human evolution
planetary revolution

every time an individual forgets
her past or her program or culture or self
even briefly
and looks at the world with new eyes
or perhaps
lives her life
in the flow
of energy
that is the universe
then that individual
is tappin' directly into the source
and allowin' that energy into the world
and it has an effect
on the whole consciousness of humanity

the right action that results from clear, clean perception
-unprejudiced-
reaches into the soul
-our common mind-
and has an effect that spreads from human to human

A Micro Event May Have a Global Effect
-witness HIV, the aids virus-
or in the brain of the human
-thought-
acts in the world
evolves quite elaborate, complex, and powerful structures
steadily increasing it's survival success
(that's the survival of thought- not necessarily it's host)
thought evolves at an exponential rate into powerful structures that
determine
the course of human affairs, individual lives, whole families, and nations
thought is a replicator in it's own right
not necessarily subservient to the original replicators
but of an altogether different order
but that's ok 'cause it comes in handy sometimes

our present diseased global culture started out like a virus
and has culminated in a cancer

and the return to health is to do nothing
let it run it's short course
and die out through perception

perception kills thought on contact
unless its the thought of the universal order
-technologic-

Better the Devil You Know
-so know your own mind-

I showed these words
to an acquaintance
who said
the person who wrote them
is deeply disturbed
obviously

and I told her
diseased
may be more apt

thought is like a virus
wholly parasitic in essence
inert outside it's host

a virus
is forever
only on the threshold of life
tiny particles of genetic material
capable of reproducing by infecting living cells
once inside the cell the virus takes over the cell's machinery
producing the virus
rather than
the cell's own chemicals

thought is like a virus

Out on the Frontier

a minority in the margins of society
-the horsemen and their god of war-
brought about our present ten thousand year old social structure

its been a minority in the margins of society
that has recently begun to change that structure
-Gandhi, X, King, Mandela-
with a passing nod to those old fellas
the so-called founding fathers
who let loose more freedom for the individual
-demanded by god's grace and instituted by men-
than any other government in the history of the world
-the USA-

now its our children
that live
at the edge of existence
in an increasingly chaotic world

its that spirit of the pioneer
out on the frontier
who expresses his or her need
for a whole life
and genuine relationship
by living beyond
the accepted boundaries
and outside the law
and includes those on the inner urban frontier
-the gangstas-
our children

why is the poor urban american
intimately involved
in the initiation
of the world's
most significant movement

Because of God's Grace Again

Out On the Inner Urban Frontier

intelligence is our common mind coming in line
with the movement of the universe

seeing evolution and tappin' that momentum

yeah
there's an inner fire burnin' just below the surface waiting to consume the
world

and if there are segments of the human population
who bear special or particular responsibility
its those who live in the USA

because of it's wealth and power and it's unique government
founded on principles of justice, liberty, and equality
-(ideals not yet fully realized, but written in law)-
based on a universe ruled by god
and because in the american urban ghetto is the greatest concentration
of intelligence on the planet
not necessarily the intelligence of school books and test scores
but the intelligence of a bone deep optimism and passion for justice
and of course
its because the wealth of the nation
that though we be laborers
under the maximum amount of stress
most of us have been fed, clothed, and sheltered
-even the unemployed-
had we been starving or malnourished too bad
intelligence would not have found
healthy human brains
continually calling out
and seeking the highest glory

if the black community
-especially in america-
is not involved
with bringing about
a planetary revolution
than it has no meaning
for anybody
anywhere

intelligence says
if it aint for everybody
it aint for anybody

everybody gonna take the role of responsibility
the opportunity
the challenge
the privilege
the demand
that life has so graciously provided

it is the human beings who live in the urban pits
who deal with the most trying situations

not only survival
food, clothing, housing, transportation, employment, health care, energy
child care, education, taxes, laws, and penalties
but what makes the burden unbearable
-CRIME-
-the question of property and psychological authority-

crime increases exponentially the burden
the crime that comes right along with the giant corporations
-our slavery to image-
the polar extreme
of the financially fit, young, healthy, blissful, beautiful,
laughing, smoking, drinking, singing, dancing, joking
images of people
pushin' product on various video screens
and radio, billboards, magazines
the images by which we judge each other
and determine our own value in the world
-absolutely and utterly false images-
produce a futile pursuit of an illusion
-a continual crime in progress-
in our mind and on the street

and in the middle of all this
the common man
tryin' ta live and do the right thing

yeah, well
the mass of humanity
be squirmin' under the thumb
of authority
both social and psychological

but wait. what was that? I forgot.
who was it we said bears the most responsibility
when faced with the present crisis
-oh yeah-
those of deeper intelligence
the poor and laboring

right. ok. well...
what about those who command the material resources of the world?
what about the stock holders and stewards of the international mega
corporations
who play global economic paper games with people's lives?
what about those who enjoy not only as complete a physical security as is
humanly possible
but also enjoy every or any other pleasure or privilege denied the common
man?

so what's up?
the degree of responsibility is in direct proportion to the degree of access
to power

the only viable social structure would be one where the head felt the pain
of the body
-which it damn sure don't now-

Intelligence Requires Tremendous Excellence and Integrity

nobody wants to hurt anybody
-naturally-
nobody wants to get hurt
but its goin' on all around us
-the hurt and the pain-

you have to be trained to be involved in that
and that trainin' goin' on all around us every day
we're in the middle of it
-grew up in it, too-
and participate right along with everybody else
-violence goin' on in all our lives_
in some form, to a certain degree
and it all comes about without our strict intention
we even turn around and scratch our head and say
with almost genuine astonishment
"look at what a mess my life/the world is! but what can I/you do?"

but what it adds up to is what we all do every day

together
all one
alone

for we alone are responsible

for stopping the cycle of violence

it is from
the urban ghettos
-the bowels of society-
that the demand is heard

and

must be answered
by those who hold
the wealth and the resources
of the most powerful
social structures
on earth

remember
-the self dies in the light of perception-
-a minority in the margins of society will change the whole-
-intelligence guides the being to health-
the force of the universe is wasted by thought making mischief
that's the self
in it's futile pursuit
of the illusion of complete physical and psychological security
because death denies all that

increase yo' access
to intelligence
and
communication
-that's love-
its right there
behind yo' eyes
an in yo' gut

intelligence commands a power
the common woman and man
or rather
what is common to the
whole of man and woman
and to the universe
the matter of substance
or rather
the substance of matter
that which has no divisions
or boundaries
that is unlimited potential
what the universe
issues from
consciousness
that is the universal energy
right there behind your eyes
understanding
the substance of the universe
consciousness
nothing
perception
the consciousness that is common to the whole of woman and man
silent and empty
vast and black
open to the movement
of universal intelligence

the revolutionary act of doing nothing

-whatever it is-

it may be
not thinking the same old thoughts
not letting the paradigm, program, presupposition, or prejudice
-the self-
run your life
it may be
not going to the job
not sending your kids to school
not watching tv
not buying or consuming alcohol or drugs
-even for a short period of time-
or tobacco or sugar or whatever
it may be
not finding fault with your mate
or not hollerin' at your kids
or not arguing or provoking your neighbor
it may be
not accepting the present corrupt social order
it may be
not thinking, but perception

observation will reveal
the world, yourself, and the right action
what not to do
and what to do
maybe any one of a million things
or all of them
or none
because there is an action
and a non action
for everybody on earth

maybe demand
a one world government
a one world currency
a one world language
so that every human being is taken into account
and allowed access to all information
and everybody has the same understanding
maybe demand whatever billions of dollars necessary
and the marshalling of resources
for the immediate development and implementation
of any and all appropriate forms of solar energy technology

maybe demand
an immediate end
to starvation and war
maybe that would be a start

maybe
talk to your family
your friends
your neighbors
far and wide

maybe
ask questions
and seek answers
relentlessly

maybe start an economic cooperative
in your local community
or a child care center
or school
or training seminars
in your area of expertise
or maybe form a temporary labor service
that treats it's employees right
maybe form a global labor union

or
maybe
sit back
and take a long look
at yourself
and the world

The Rich White Folks Downtown

I don't think the big wigs runnin' things
gonna volunteer to create new systems
of service and production and distribution

"They" Aint Gonna Do It
I call 'em big wigs 'cause they heads so big
they actually believe
and live their lives
as if they were better than us
while we go right along with it
-puttin' on a front-
but on the inside we're angry, sad, fearful, and hungry

the big wigs aint gonna change nothin'
-they have the power and control-
you think they gonna give it up voluntarily?
hell no!
we can't look to them to do right any longer
-there's no more time-
a gradual change is unacceptable
its been gradual for far too long
besides, the only change I been seein'
is the rich gettin' richer and the poor poorer

I don't think the big wigs runnin' things
is gonna make sure
everybody ok

all I'm sayin' is
intelligence
individual and collective
local and global
is demanded
by the present crisis

all your senses wide open
observing the world
our self, society, and the environment
without fear
and unobstructed by thought

hey! still tryin' ta catch holt to it-

its that one movement of perception
that precedes whatever the particular neural firing pattern
-memory, comparison, judgment, etc.-
that associates with whatever the sensory input is

its that space between thoughts
its that elusive instant of integrity
and it cannot be captured by thought

its that space in which thought appears
you can see it right there
in the interval between your own thoughts

intelligence may come not only through observation but through
communication
intelligence occurs spontaneously as an inherent feature of a healthy
human brain
and it *may* be transmitted to other brains as *new* knowledge
the effect of *new* knowledge on a human brain, transmitted culturally,
may not be as potent
as one's own immediate penetrating perception, but new knowledge may
be intelligent
long as its uncorrupted by the self

perceive the symbol, then observe that to which it refers

the seed of full consciousness is the ability to observe
your own thought processes at work
how they affect your action
and how they are transformed by observation

where they come from and where they goin'

139

to plant a seed in the mind of man

it is our intention
to transform
how the brain presently functions
as regards the process of thought
that determines our behavior

it is our intention to bring about a radical revolution in the consciousness
of humanity
and thereby in the world

not by introducing a particular thought, phrase, sound bite, belief, or
image
but by helping to bring about a simple awareness
of what's goin' on
both inwardly, psychologically and outwardly, socially and environmentally
and the relationship thereof

there is only one action necessary
and from that action issues forth the revolution

to see the whole of what is

observation without fear or prejudice

a clear, clean observation reveals
the action or non action
that a whole life demands

when the self dies
there is no authority
to tell ya what to do

so just look and see

and do and be

The End of Thought
its like all aspects of health
-when its workin' right ya don't hafta think about it-

it happens naturally, effortlessly
-the brain uses 20% of the body's energy-
when you're livin' fully conscious
its a whole lot easier
gettin' through the day
without a whole lotta energy wasted
on thinkin 'bout
a bunch of memories, dreams, fears, etc.
hopes and regrets and on and on
all bouncin' off each other
triggerin' a multitude of others
and repeating cycles and patterns
same as the day before

yeah, the day goes by better when you're fully attentive and aware
the work goes smooth 'cause ya right there guidin' the work the right way
-naturally-smoothly-easily-
its not like ya turn into a zombie and can't remember ya phone number
or your kid's birthday or how ta do ya job

but the end of thought may allow ya ta forget why ya sometimes get ta
feelin' not so good

It Aint So Easy
yeah, well, laborin' at the low wage jobs
often at least one or more bad conditions such as
extreme heat or cold, loud noise, dust, dirt, grease, blood, noxious fumes
dangerous equipment and tools and procedures
monotonous, repetitive work
little or no relationship between work performed and wage earned

the big wigs don't give a damn 'bout ya!
-and ya betta believe it baby!-

141

I've Did This and I've Did That

I really wanted to avoid this part, but it may help some folks understand this book a little better, so here it goes real quick. The less said about my youth and first few years after attaining 'legal' age the better. At some point in my mid twenties I made a conscious decision to do right and live healthy. Whether or not I have been successful at that is open to question, but I have definitely strived to the best of my ability to support myself and my family within the boundaries of what is morally and legally correct. This been goin' on now for 'bout twenty years.

I haven't had too much trouble finding work. I've worked in every aspect of the chicken industry from hatching to slaughtering- hogs, too- I've cleaned the kill floor and the holding pens, I've built furniture and houses, I've worked in beau coup machine shops and warehouses, I've picked strawberries with the migrant workers (and from that experience I gathered the impression that women and children in third world countries work harder than men do in the industrialized nations), I made a hand in the oil fields, and I've worked in mills of wood, metal, plastic, and video tape. And I'd estimate twenty percent of that work been through temporary labor companies.

During these years I've talked to and worked with and lived side by side with a whole lotta folks in the same boat as me and brother I'm here to tell ya, it aint easy- the pain and humiliation of livin' in poverty. If we gotta work anyway, why not work to create a new world?

A World Wide Network

We can create the network that will balance out large scale integration. The population explosion and the exploitation of world resources- human and material- requires that large scale integration take place- our connection to our brothers and sisters all over the world. Our interconnectedness is actual. Large scale integration establishes the structure for our communication and exchange of energy, material, and the distribution of wealth- while the network establishes the human sensitivity to human need. The network is based on human contact at the level of the common man- not the level of the fortified disneyland castles of the ruling elite high on the hill. Human contact- that's the single most valuable facet of human life- the higher the quality of contact, the richer, the deeper, the healthier the life.

In the network there is no single authority that dominates. The power of the network is in the healthy values and intention of goodness shared by all. The network doesn't demand everyone agree on every detail or follow the same course of action. It allows individuals and organizations to work together and share information and resources. It allows all to explore their own potentials and possibilities. It allows ideas and influence to spread naturally without demanding adherence to a particular code of conduct. It allows for adaptation, change, and evolution. Individual's and organization's goals and objectives may overlap or remain separate, to be specific or general, local and /or global as the case may be.

The network is based on human contact- the need for help and the willingness to help, economically, materially, socially, psychologically, informationally. Talk to people, ask for assistance, commit to assist, organize and experiment and follow through. See and let yourself be seen.

Karma and the Golden Rule

true human contact
healthy human contact
yeah
ya know
its governed by
by that one
Universal Law of Human Relationship
-LOVE-

is that too sappy for ya
sorry
its just one of those laws of the universe
ya can't get around
like gravity, breathing, and death

-THE ONE LAW-
do unto others as you would have them do unto you
-Jesus-

or

make haste and do what is good, keep your mind away from evil
-Buddha-

Who Knows?
-what to do-

the people out there doin' it
on the floor
in the street
out in the fields
and in the trenches
-that's us-
that be workin' every day
we know
-just ask-
its right there in front of our faces

and the ones locked in their boxes
-that's them-
downtown
runnin' things
they don't know and they don't care

they don't know a radical change is required
they don't care a radical change is demanded
and they don't care that they don't know

the armageddon that's fixin' ta happen
is between
the defender's of authority and the concept of property- slavery
and those free people who see
that health and security are human rights
too long denied- freedom and justice

and the warriors action is guided by the one law

yes, a revolutionary will encounter resistance
yes, the inevitable conflict will be ended immediately
and
yes, the appropriate action will be within the one law

warriors, armageddon, and the one law of love
yeah
the reason it sounds contradictory
is because we are violent
our planetary culture is violent
we are trained to accept violence as a way of life
and violence begets violence

its the one law of love that denies violence
its the love that demands goodness
and being good is understanding
and understanding is being fully conscious
and consciousness, being not a thing- nothing- can offer no resistance
and violence encountering no resistance
produces no reaction
has nowhere to go
nothing to do
serves no purpose
gains nothing and stops

intelligence declares
food, clothing, shelter
-physical security-
and free access to information, material, and energy
-products of the universe-
are human rights
because the goddess
didn't give birth to the world
for the exclusive benefit of the rich white folks downtown
but she did create the world
as a blessing and a grace
for the whole human being

BOOK NINE

That's a Whole Lotta Folks
that's everybody and they all around us
and we're right in the middle of 'em

I can't have a whole lotta everything
a hundred times more than I'll actually need in a life time
without a thousand of you and your families sacrificing whole lifetimes
strugglin' in pain day after day, year in and year out
-that's called responsibility-

when the poor laborers have met their responsibility by goin' to work
every day
for the miserly pay the rich folks decide on
the miserly pay that determines the poor folks whole quality of life and
human relations
then what relationship have the rich to the poor?
are the rich and powerful simply masters according to manifest destiny?
how long will the poor accept this relationship?

master and slave, rich and poor
this problem been at the core of human existence
ever since the violent been takin' slaves

its all about a violation of human rights
and
a global crime in progress
and
it all hinges on this
whether or not there is such a thing as human rights
-either there is or there aint-

if there is
they apply to all humanity

if there aint no such thing as human rights
then we need to establish human rights
as planetary law

ok
so if the truth be known
human rights are recognized
in thought
but not in actuality

the most dramatic
and well known
is that document
that is the very
spirit and symbol
of freedom
in the world

the declaration of independence

these few words say it all
"...in the course of human events, it becomes necessary...
for people
...to assume...
the
...equal station...
which the laws of nature and
...nature's god entitle them...
these truths
...be self evident...
all men are created equal
...they are endowed by their creator with certain unalienable rights...
among these are life, liberty, and the pursuit of happiness
...to secure these rights governments are instituted...
deriving their just powers from the consent of the governed
...whenever...
government becomes destructive of these ends
it is the right of the people to alter or abolish it"

was the word property mentioned there?
no

basically what it says is- GOD GIVEN HUMAN RIGHTS ARE DEMANDED!
the actual course human events have taken has been in the opposite
direction- the establishment, expansion, and protection of property rights
rather than human rights

the one law that denies all authority

the voices in yo' head
from within and without
parental voices and police
poets, priests, and politicians
-denied-

the one law
comes from within and without
-like a pulse or vibration-
first observing clearly the world
then the response of your own mind

the one law
is established
in the silence and space of perception
-an intense awareness inwardly and outwardly-
and expands through right human relationship
action born of the love and compassion
that is the unlimited energy of the universe
-a clear, clean conscience-
human consciousness unburdened by the self

ONE WORLD - ONE LAW

Being Fully Conscious
is gathering energy and bringing order
that's what the whole organism wants to do anyway
be healthy and function wholly
as the universe intended when it evolved the human being
being fully conscious
is facing death
the death of the self
the end of thought
is lining up the whole organism with the movement of the universe
it don't mean pleasure, it may be pain and sacrifice
but if the organism is functioning in harmony with the whole energy of the
universe
that's when you sense the world and people and your whole life most
intimately
it don't necessarily mean ecstatic psychological experience
but it does mean
that the insights and knowledge and materials and energy
relevant to you and me and the world's healing and health arise
naturally, appropriately, spontaneously, and unexpectedly
from within and without
'cause we're bein' carried by the flow of the universe
-that's intelligence-

we can't bring about
the obvious change needed
by steady doin' the same things
over and over
-thinkin' the same thoughts-

the most relevant, significant action
may be to do nothing
and observe everything
the whole environment
and how everything affects everything else

its like that old so called philosophical question of fate and free will
it only comes out of thought's confusion
the innate contradiction- the paradox
the inherent inability of symbols to convey wholeness

perception has not that misunderstanding

If You Do What I Say, You Will Have Faced Death
sit down
in a quiet place
observe your environment
then close your eyes
and observe
the process of thought
and
what happens next
do it
for three minutes
or thirty
or an hour or two
or when you're under stress
or when you're happy and feelin' good
or for a lifetime

that's putting thought in it's proper place
the fear of death
the impediment of life
exists only in thought
-that's the self-

Full Consciousness
is the direct and immediate connection
between intelligence and the human being
there is no authority
that will solve the world's problems
or the problems of the individual for that matter
and one thing's for sure
we can't just keep takin' the same actions or variations over and over
and expect a good outcome
the correct action is unknown
'cause its not from the past
the correct action can only be lived each moment
through simple observation of what is

simple observation requires an excellent mind
not a mind that becomes a Rhodes scholar or enters Harvard or M.I.T.
but a mind that doesn't give up
in the face of hardship, extreme prejudice, or fear

The Child is Born in Paradise

that's what having a clean, unconditioned mind is like
-heaven-

the child grows out of a world
of which the child is the fruit
a world of perfection
and exact proportion
for the human being to thrive

and it is we
who introduce
the child
to the hell
of human society

that's worse than a mere crime
-that's an abomination-

Let the Children Go

stop creating
in them
an image
of god
'cause as soon as the mind symbolizes
-*that*-
it cuts itself off
from immediate, direct contact
channeling the brain's energy into a dead end
-it stops perception-

Free the Children

stop creating in them images
lest they be swallowed by
the most powerful authority of all
-THOUGHT-
is a replicator
that demands
eternal vigilance
because
prejudice lives
in the mind of man

afterwords

revolutions be occurring
all over the globe
and nobody notices
much less cares
but a revolution
occurring in the u.s.
will be felt worldwide

and the first order of business
must be to clean up
the corrosive residue of evil
perpetrated in the past

lastword

I acknowledge
Richard Dawkins and J. Krishnamurti
thanx

About the Author

Syndax Vuzz is not an expert in any recognized field of study.

After one year of college and seven years traveling the states from California to Florida working farms, factories, machine shops, warehouse, construction and the oil fields Vuzz settled down to over two decades of providing for a family on the wages of a common laborer.

All the while, one burning obsession possessed his mind- revolution, both psychological and social- how to live a free, creative, righteous life in the middle of the cutthroat competition of the urban consumer economy.

The voice of Syndax Vuzz carries the weight and authority of the common man, the mass of humanity and speaks for those in pain.

www.ingramcontent.com/pod-product-compliance
Lightning Source LLC
Chambersburg PA
CBHW020427290526
45785CB00002B/735